THE SORROWS OF A SHOW GIRL: A STORY OF THE GREAT "WHITE WAY"

By

KENNETH McGAFFEY

The Sorrows Of A Show Girl:
A Story Of The Great "White Way"

by **Kenneth McGaffey**

ISBN: 978-93-57481-93-9

Published by

DOUBLE 9 BOOKS

2/13-B, Ansari Road, Daryaganj
New Delhi – 110002
info@double9books.com
www.double9books.com
Tel. 011-40042856

ABOUT THE AUTHOR

Kenneth McGaffey is an author who wrote only one book in his entire life. McGaffey published A Story Of The Great "White Way" in 1908. This book belongs to fictional genre. A Story Of The Great "White Way" by Kenneth McGaffey has been out for print for decades and therefor has not been accessible to the general public.

CONTENTS

EXPLANATION.

In the following chapters some of Sabrina's remarks are likely to cause the reader to elevate his eyebrows in suspicion as to her true character.

In order to set myself right with both the public and the vast army of Sabrinas that add youth and beauty to our stage, and brilliancy and gaiety to our well known cafes, I wish to say that she is all that she should be. She is a young lady who, no matter how old she may be, does not look it. She is always well dressed, perhaps a little in advance of the fashion, but invariably in good taste. Among strangers or in public places her conduct is all that could be desired, while with those of her own set she becomes more familiar and may occasionally lapse into slang.

Fate may compel her to earn her own living or she may receive an income from a source that has nothing to do with these stories. Any person without the circle of theatrical or newspaper life is looked upon as an interloper by Sabrina and treated accordingly. Hundreds of her like may be found any evening after the theatre in the cafes and restaurants of the "wiseacres" known as the "Tenderloin."

KENNETH MCGAFFEY.

In which Sabrina rushes on the scene and begins to discourse breathlessly on theatrical conditions, boobs that send poetry for presents, the tribulations of hunting employment, and the outlook for a New Year's dinner.

CHAPTER ONE

"Ain't it appalling," demanded Sabrina, the Show Girl, "ain't it appalling the way the show game has gone to the morgue this season?

"I never seen nothing like it since I been in the business, and while I ain't going to flash no family Bible that's been some time. Why, shows that were making money if they played to thirty-two dollars on the day just naturally died. Me? You know I wasn't hep to the outlook. I come prancing into town fresh from doing one-night stands through the uncultured West. We did bum business for fair, but shucks, there ain't five dollars' worth of real money in all of Southern Kansas at no time. Salaries! Huh! I had to send home for money to pay my fines with. I cavort gaily out to hunt a job and find a line from Mr. Seymour's office that made the run on the Knickerbocker Trust Company look like the nightly window sale of 'The Evangelist.' I never seen so many of my friends in town at one time in my life, and if you make a noise like a dollar-bill anywhere between the two Flatirons you're liable to be the center of a raging mob. I heard it breathed that all the theatrical storehouses in town were playing to S.R.O.

"I got a chance to shake down a little change as prima donna with a turkey show. What do you know about that? I played with one last Thanksgiving, and—excuse these tears—it was a college town and the show was on the blink. 'Nough said. The manager hasn't left there yet.

"Oh, Listerine, have you heard the news? Alia McGraw has turned poetess. You know she always was peculiar. I was visiting her the other evening in her dressing room when she declared that she was going to give up her dramatic art and go to painting word pictures. Whatever they are. You see it was this way: She had a boob on her staff who was paying her his devoted attention. According to her statistics that's all he ever did pay for. Well, he commenced doing advance work about a present he was going to give her until he got poor Alla to thinking that it was nothing less than an automobile, and she treated him accordingly. One morning a messenger boy makes his entrance into the flat and hands her a book. Can you beat that? The only thing that kept Alia from foaming at the mouth was because she was combing her Dutch braid. It—the book—was called a Rubaiyat by Omar Quinine, or something like that. This Omar party never wrote a comic opera in his life. But Alla wasn't discouraged, for she looked through every page in hopes of finding a Clearing House certificate, but not a leaf stirred. All she came across was a marked verse that went something like this:

> "A book of verse underneath a bough,
> A Jug of wine, a loaf of bread and thou
> Beside me sitting in the wilderness—
> Oh, wilderness is Paradise enow.

"Did you ever hear of such a short sport? Wanted to buy it by the keg and go sit under a tree in Bronx Park. As soon as Alla run out of language she sat down and in less than three hours doped out an answer. I got it here on the back of her laundry list:

> "A book of verse is not what I can use,
> But give me, if still my love is thine,
> A wine list from which to pick and choose.
> Cut out the shady bough for mine.

> "Give your bough to some nice 'feller,'
> And if you would make my life sublime
> Put me in some cool rathskeller
> And we'll forget the jug of wine.

> "Wine in a jug! What do I hear?
> Not with a loaf of bread and thou,
> A cheese sandwich and a glass of beer,
> Unless you've changed your brand ere now.

> "This sitting in the wilderness may be fine
> For those who the realms of nature seek,
> A restaurant is at least a paradise divine
> With payday on the first of every week.

"I guess maybe that won't show him up! Ain't it just glorious? It's kinda wabbly on its feet, but just think, it's her first attempt. She said there were a lot more things she could say, but even her desire to be a poetess wouldn't let her forget that she was a lady. Alla told me that the height of her ambition was to write the words of a popular song and have Harry Von Seltzer sing it in the College Inn. She can't ever make a hit as a poem producer though 'cause she hasn't got high cheek bones and teeth like a squirrel. Alla was pensive all through the first act, and while she was making her change from a lady-in-waiting to a bathing girl she remarked that she was going to write an ode—past tense of I O U, I guess—entitled 'Thoughts on Hearing Ben Teal Conduct a Chorus Rehearsal.' They won't let her publish it.

"What do you know about the new law about tanks having to have their names on the barroom door? I see where the Metropole will lose money unless they furnish disguises to their steady customers. Can you imagine the suspense certain parties will feel when they rush into a shop for their early morning 'thought mop' and have to cling to the bar while Arthur looks up their past performances in Bingham's Bartenders' Guide.

"A gentleman friend had the kindness to extend me courtesies to 'The Witching Hour' the other evening, and listen to muh: There is some class to that show. Ain't you seen it? It's a song and dance about this mental telepathy gag. There is a gambling gentleman who can tell a poker hand every time. The only reason he ain't a heiress is because his conscience jumps up and gives him a kick in the face. This party in the play influences people's minds. He thinks of something, and people miles away think of the same thing. All the same wireless. Take it from me, there's a whole lot to it at that. I was out with a kind friend the other evening whose general disposition is to try and make Frank Daniels look like a spendthrift, so I knew it would be beer for mine unless I made a great mental effort, so all the way up the street in the taxicab I just held thumbs and concentrated my mind—I saw more new style hats, too—and said to myself, 'For Heaven's sake, order wine,' 'Please loosen up and order wine.' All to myself, you understand, never once out loud, for though I am in the business I don't seek the reputation as a working girl.

"Well I hope I may never look a lobster in the face again. No, I am not speaking of this party. But I hope I may never look a lobster in the face again if he didn't swell all up, prance into the eat hut and say careless like over his shoulder to the waiter, 'A bottle of that Brut.' Just like that. I tried the concentration gag on him for a pearl ring he had on, thinking I had him under the gypsy curse, but there was a person who had the nerve to call herself a lady who had been saying things about me sitting at another table with a Harry who had led me to believe that I was his own little Star of Hope, and I just couldn't get my mind centered.

"Honest to goodness, I don't know what I'll do unless I find work. My suite of apartments is reduced now to one hall room and a closet, and the Dennett & Child's circuit is beginning to look like K. & E. booking. The only thing I can think of for me to do is to get engaged and hock the betrothal ring for a meal ticket.

"Me for roller skates. Here I've been hunting a job until I wore out two pair of these Sorosis things and not a bush shakes. Can't even sign a contract for a Friday night amateur contest. By gum, I'd take a job barking for a snake race. I had an offer to go into vaudeville. What do you know about that? The act hasn't any time yet, but it will get time as soon as it makes good, and to make good all its needs is a trial performance, and the backer thinks he knows where he can get a trial performance, and to get ready for the trial performance will require about five weeks' rehearsal at nix per week. Do you think a stunt like that is worthy of my attention? Adversity does sure land on the poor chorus doll with both feet at every stage of the game.

"I was reading in the paper the other day that some old pappy guy out in Chi was making a noisy fuss that the chorus ladies stay up too late nights. I wish somebody would show him to me, that's all I ask, just show him to me. I suppose old Pink Whiskers was a chorus man once himself and has got all the dope on the subject. So we stay up late, do we? I suppose he will be wanting us to read helpful books instead of making up, next. To my mind, of course I may be wrong, but to my mind the staying up late nights ain't half as bad as getting up in the morning. Of course, I don't know who or what this old wop is that made this crack, but if he thinks we spend most of our time in sinful idleness he'd better copper his bet. All we do is rehearse all morning, matinee all afternoon, performance all evening and travel all night. The rest of the time we have to ourselves, and he thinks we frivol. Why, he ain't wise to half the privations they force on us. Would you believe it? I have gone forty weeks without never even catching a glimpse of Broadway, and once went for ten without even a cheese sandwich to bring gladness to my heart. Can you beat that? And then he goes and turns loose a rebel yell because when we do get a little time to ourselves we stay up late nights. Oh, Mellen's Food! When does he want us to stay up? Mornings? Some wise boy once said, 'Early to bed, early to rise, but you don't meet any prominent people,' and I guess maybe he wasn't right. He got the number then all right, all right, and he didn't have to speak harsh to Central at that. We gotta do something to amuse ourselves, and I never had a traveling gentleman yet conduct me to a watch meeting. A girl comes out of the stage door tired and lonesome; some village cut-up prances out and gets acquainted; the girl is hungry, so why not? Perhaps she is sending money home every week and can't afford a little lunch after the show herself. No, that's no taproom jest. There is more than one of the merry-merry putting her little sister through school and don't you forget it for a minute. And he gets sore because we stay up late nights. He'd better roll another pill, get at the cause and then hang the curfew on a few of those town romps. If he hands out another song and dance number like that again, send him up to me, I'll give him a bunch of inside info that will make him think something broke loose.

"I managed to slip in and see 'The Talk of New York' the other night. Say, that's a great play. Did you get wise to the way that Kid Burns party juggles the loose talk? I don't believe there ever was a party that slings slang the way that guy does. My mother was always particular about my bringing up, and if I ever passed out any of this George Cohan style of repartee she would give me a slap on the map and tell me to chase back and handle my harangue as per Mr. Webster. So, though I have traveled about a bit, I still retain my pure English, even when I lose my temper, which is going some for a lady.

"What am I going to do New Year's? I know one thing. I ain't going to play an encore to the sozzle session number I pulled off last season. Didn't you hear about it? Evidently you were not on Broadway last New Year's Eve. A couple of young ladies and myself were playing a progressive hell party all up and down the main street. You see, you play it this way. A guy comes up and blows a horn in your ear. You swat the horn quickly on the end with your hand. If the guy swallows more than half the horn you win and are allowed to 'phone for the ambulance. But that was only a prelude to the main event. Ah, me! I blush to chronicle it. There were so many shows in town that the supply of college students didn't come up to the demand, and as me and the bunch had sorta turned them down after they went and lost all their money on the Thanksgiving game, so we had an intimation that developed into a hunch that our little 'welcome' mat on the doorstep would not be crowded with an eager throng. We engaged a couple of window tables at the Cafe des Beaux Minks realizing that though we were not in the money we were still on the track. This was last New Year's Eve. New Year's afternoon we held a reception up at Miss Verneaque's flat, took up a collection for the widows and orphans and cleared $4.43 apiece on it. The place got pinched and we all had to hide on the roof until the cops beat it. But not for me this year. Me for the peaceful kind of a celebration. I don't know what to do. The only people I have on my calling list now are the agents, and they will all be home splashing in the egg-nog.

"Gee, but I wish I was home. Was you ever in a country town on a New Year's Day? Say, list. Sixty laughs in sixty minutes looks like a busy day at the morgue compared to the laughs they hand out in one of those one-night stand dumps. The Sons of Temperance all go out and get a bun on ad lib. and everybody inhales good cheer. I sang in the choir. Honest I did, but it didn't take. I got a silver cigarette case yet the choirmaster gave me. But no home this year; me to the Cafe des Enfants. What? Will I? Don't make such a foolish noise. I'll be there with my hair in a braid. Two-thirty at Hector's. Say, you've got the Good Samaritan looking like a rent collector. So long."

In which Sabrina discloses a little of her past and those of the members of the company, tells how she was a bridesmaid and goes into detail in regard to the benefit to humanity of having carrier pigeons trained to rush the growler.

CHAPTER TWO

I was strolling down Broadway the other afternoon with Oscar when we happened to meet Miss Sabrina, the show girl. I introduced them, of course, and then retired to the background. This is what followed:

"I am very glad to meet you, Mr. Jenkins. I've heard the party here speak of you."

"Yes; and I have heard him say several nice things about you."

"Is that so?"

"Sure. But don't take it to heart; he means well."

"Well, I can only say he treats me like a true friend."

"Speaking of treats, I'll buy the beer."

"My goodness! Ain't you afraid of catching cold—taking so much money out of your clothes all at once?"

"What was that you handed out? Come again, please."

"I merely remarked that it was awful kind of you."

"Oh, that's all right; I always was careless with my money."

"I always like this place; it reminds me so much of the back of the drug store in Emporia."

"Then you are from the West, Miss De Vear."

"Oh, yes, indeed, I'm a Western girl pure and simple—"

"You said, 'pure and simple,' did you not?"

"I most certainly did, and I'd like to see the party that's got anything on me. I come from a dead swell family, I do. I may be only a poor chorus girl, but by gosh! I was brung up right. Did you know that I was featured for three seasons in the church choir in my home town and would have had it for life if the stage manag—I mean the choirmaster hadn't forgot he was a gentleman; so I just quit rather than cause talk. Why, would you believe it?—my father was mayor of Emporia for nearly two terms. You'd be surprised if I told you my real name and some of the people I am related to. Say, what are you going to do with that book? Trying to dope out whether you can buy another drink, I suppose."

"No. I'm just keeping track of the girls I met whose fathers are mayors of towns. I've got forty-seven for Providence, R.I., fifteen for Peoria, Ill., ten for Atlanta, Ga., and your two makes seven for Emporia. I've got fifty-three for chief of police, twenty-one fire captains, and eleven postmas—"

"Excuse me, but are you trying to infer that I am telling an untruth?"

"Oh, forget it! Can't you stand a little jolly without going up in the air?"

"Well, I'll accept your apology, but I don't like to have people casting slurs on my pa and ma, and beer wont appease my wrath when I feel like a highball.

"Go as far as you like. I was only ordering what I thought you were accustomed to."

"Say, Mr. Percival B. Fresh, you certainly are the village wag when it comes to the Oriental repartee, ain't you?"

"Sure I am, but I have to go to the mat when they commence to dish out this Emporia humor. Oh. Laza! Do you care for the one in red?"

"Of course I may go wrong, but in my mind no gentleman would make remarks about another girl when he is with a lady."

"Say, girlie, you're all right—lovely hair, beautiful eyes and all that—but cut it; drop in your penny and get wise to yourself. That's a great show you are with."

"When was you out front?"

"Night before last."

"Night before last! My Heavens! Wasn't I a sight? You know the girl I dress with had been out to a wine supper and she came splashing into the dressing room lit up like a show window and cried my makeup box full of tears over the death of her baby sister, and the way I had to put it on I thought was sure good for a fine, and to make matters worse some hussy got next to all my toothpicks and I had to use a hairpin for a liner; but did you notice the way that cat of a soubrette keeps me out of the spotlight? Professional jealousy, that's all; but it don't do me no good to kick, because the stage manager sends her silk stockings and that kind of junk, while the best I get is a chance to hold hands with the electrician; but, of course, he gets his orders."

"Say, that piece of work that stands on the end opposite you is all to the berries, ain't she?"

"Her!"

"Surest thing you know. She looks like a night-blooming pippin to me."

"My, gracious, Mr. Jenkins, I never knocked a living soul, but I don't mind telling you as a friend that I personally would not degrade myself by speaking to her, and of course you know that the hair she wears is not her own. I haven't a thing in the world against the poor creature, but it has been breathed around the company that she is not all she should be. Of course, I don't know positively, but it is what everybody says, and I only wish she would make good with that four bits of mine."

"Well, I'm glad there's no hard feeling between you two, as I would like to meet her."

"I'm very sorry, but you will have to pardon me if I refuse to give you a knockdown, for I would steer no friend of a friend of mine up against a flim flam where there's so many nice girls running loose. Take Tessie Samonies, for example, she ain't very pretty, but she's awfully cute, and after she gets a couple of sloe gins boosted into her she certainly is the life of the party."

"All right, frame it up for me and I'll open wine or a window or something to show that I'm a true sport."

"You bet I will, and we'll have a nice little family party, no knocking or nothing; just sit and talk real friendly like."

"That's the idea and if anyone starts the anvil chorus they get the skiddo. What? Who will we have?"

"Well, let's see, we'll have Tessie and you, me and Silent Murphy here— and let's see who else?"

"Joe Zeweibaum and Miss Veronique."

"Not yet. Joe is all right in a crowd if you can keep him from talking about his sales, but the dame—not for me, for if there's any one gets my goat she's it."

"Shall we have Frank Millar and his first wife?"

"Oh, heavings! No! For if we did his third wife would hear about it and then she would knock me to my husband, for you know they are engaged, so if she hears anything about me you can bet she plays it up strong."

"Well, can't you think of some one else?"

"No, I don't know a soul that is any good but us four. My goodness, I've got to roll my hoop and do a shopping number, get my hair gargled—I slept in it last night—and see a sick friend.

"Fate sure does sic tribulations on me at every turn of the road. This business of hunting employment has got to be so balmy that I snort and jump sideways every time anybody says 'job.'

"Now that the first of the year has kicked in, I thought everything would be as merry as a marriage bell, but as yet there hasn't been a ripple on the water. The only thing that acts as a star of hope to my miserable existence is a date with a Summer stock that opens the first of June, and there is a heap of smoke around that. I wish some one would tip me off to some way of earning an honest living without having to resort to a sock full of sand or a strong arm. But why be downhearted? I haven't drunk up all my Christmas presents yet. As a last hope I can load upon them and get some kind ambulance to drag me up to the dippy department of some nice hospital. Honest, I am getting so thin that before long I won't be able to understudy a drop of water in Mr. Hawk's Hippodrome.

"A nice gentleman presented himself to me on Broadway the other evening and, after passing the compliments of the season, invited me out to inhale a young table d'hote. The way I sprang to his side made a leap for life seem like sinful idleness. And where do you think he took me? I ask as a friend, Where do you think he took me? To one of those joints where you get everything from soup to nuts, including a scuttle full of red ink for thirty-five scudi. I was going to balk and rear in the harness when he started to lead me up the steps of the foundry, but as I always maintained discretion is the better part of valor, I'm two-bits ahead anyway you play it. So I climb into the nosebag without a peep. Yet—would you believe it?—when that wop came to cash in he shook the mothballs out of a roll of bills that looked like nine miles' worth of hall carpet. I had been acting very reserved heretofore, but when he made this flash he commenced to look like a very dear friend of mine who had been very kind to me in moments of adversity. I apprised him of the fact, and the dog had the temerity to pin his pocket shut with a safety pin right before my eyes. I come to find out later that he was a press agent. Ain't it scandalous the way the Friars wine and dine the dramatists every few weeks? I tried to agitate a bunch for the chorus girls to give a dinner to Ben Teal or William Seymour, but while they were all willing to be in on the big eat the way they ducked the financial responsibilities would have made you think it was a half-salary clause.

"The other day I put my ear to the ground and then cavorted madly around to Mr. Savage's office to see if there was anything doing in the 'Merry Widow' line. The handsome gentleman on the other side of the desk allowed a ripple of merriment to float over his features and then spake as follows: 'All we got to do is to toll the bell in the old church tower and nine companies will answer like the fire department.' You know I could have gone with the Paris 'Prince of Pilson' company, but those French gentlemen are so emotional. One tried to bite my ear in Jack's the other night.

"Did I tell you about Mamie de Vere becoming a bride again? She believes in marrying at leisure and divorcing in haste. The justice of the peace that always ties her nuptial knot told her that if she bought a ticket she could save 50 cents per wedding and he would hand it to the happy bridegroom as her dowry. Well, anyway they got maried after the show, so that she wouldn't loose her job. I was maid of honor. Honest I was. Don't it sound funny? And I carried her bouquet as the bridal party marched up the hall to the office of the justice of the peace. Just as he was about to pronounce the last sad rites a hurdy-gurdy started playing 'Don't Get Married Any More, Ma,' with variations. Well, it made Mamie so nervous. You know she always was a hysterical creature. It made her so nervous that she had to have Wilbur— that's her husband—go out and put a bug on the Ginny before she would allow the flag to drop. Then we went out and had our wedding breakfast. There were six or eight in the crowd, I don't rightly remember which, for sometimes there would be only a few and then again it would be a turbid throng.

"A couple of whisky sales gentlemen joined our little gathering and proposed a race. You know I do so love athletic sports. I don't mean prize fighters or ball players, but feats of strength. The whisky gentlemen had a little the best start, for they had been running trial heats. The way we staged that drinking number was a crime. How we ended up I care not, neither do I spin. I can merely state that Mamie and I slid for home in a sea-going taxicab, leaving Wilbur saying things to the head waiter that no lady would listen to.

"Oh, say, are you here with any extra junk? No, this ain't no touch. But if you have got a reckless bundle I know how you can double it in a few weeks. A gentleman friend of mine was captain of a fake wire-tapping game until he got put out of business by the hard times and the lack of suckers—synonymous. He is selling stock of a proposition that has anything from Goldfield chased back to the desert. This is the scheme: Listerine. He's going to train carrier pigeons to rush the growler. The Chorus Girls' Union have already elected him an honorary vice-president. You see, he gets these birds and trains them to carry the pail in their teeth and smell out the nearest saloon, even a blind tiger—no matter where they are. Then he rents the birds out by the dozen to the theatrical organizations—special rates to musical comedies—so that all the poor merry-merry has to do if there is no gentleman without is get a bird from the property man, beat it for the furnished room, drop ten cents in the bucket, write a little note to the bartender merely stating: 'Mother has company, so not so much foam, please,' open the window and start the dove of peace on its mission of happiness. You needn't be afraid of the pigeon sneaking up an alley and drinking half of it and then coming back with the stall, 'The boss is on tonight; there ain't no bellhop to tip and all the bird wants is three or four grains of corn, mother, and its just as happy and care free as if you opened wine. Won't that be a boon to humanity, though? If he don't get a Carnegie medal things are run wrong. Another stunt he is going to pull off is canned cheese sandwiches. Well, I got to toddle along. The Ladies' Auxiliary to the Anvil Chorus is going to hold a meeting in Alla Sweenie's apartments. Was you ever one of them? Well, when those dames get on the job and are grouped it makes Elinor Glyn's opinion of the Pilgrim Mothers seem like words of praise. So long."

In which Sabrina receives money from an unexpected source, and brings to light how she came to receive it and what she intends doing when the entire sum is given her.

CHAPTER THREE

"Providence has got to throw something besides 'crap,' some time or other," remarked Sabrina, the show girl as we complimented her upon her new gown. "And I guess I am there with rings on my fingers and bells on my toes, or words to that effect. Take me by the hand and lead me to some secluded nook and I will unburden my young soul."

When we had seated ourselves and the waiter had retired for the second time she began:

"You have been hearing me put up a plaintive plea about being on the rocks. Well, I was. I had everything in hock but my self-respect, and I had that ready to tuck under my shawl at a moment's notice and rush off to Uncle Sim's. But never again for muh. I was up in my suite wondering if I could sign checks at Child's when the landlady shoved a letter under my door—she could have shoved a dog under just as well as not. I dive for the epistle, thinking, perhaps, it is some word of encouragement from Matt Grau. I tear open the envelope and pull out a letter and out drops a piece of paper that could look like it meant money. It's a cinch I beat it to the floor. It was a check. I staggered against the gas stove I was so surprised; then I unfolded it and it was made out to me. Can you beat that? To me, and in my real name, for one hundred, count 'em, one hundred cold, hard Clearing House certificates. The only thing that kept me from having a scene with myself was the fact that I had drank up all my merry Yuletide gifts. Well, by and by, after piping off the check, counting it, biting it, smelling it, I had sense enough to look at the letter. This is going to be a long, sad tale, so you had better—yes, that's it—a little more of the same. You see, it was this way.

"Last season when I—thank goodness—when I was with a Broadway production instead of a road show, a certain party, whom I had met while out on the one-night stands the season before, came stampeding into town and it fell upon my fair young shoulders to show him the sights. Query—Did I show him the sights? Answer—Yes, I did show him the sights. If there was any place we didn't see it was because you had to have an introduction to get in.

"Then Edward became inoculated with an idea that it would be a good plan to consume all the booze on Broadway, thereby preventing others from living intemperate lives. Such a chance. You know the new tunnel couldn't hold the reserve supply of liquids that can report for duty at a minute's notice on the corner of Forty-second and Broadway. The first time I got hep to those proceedings was when I received the glad tidings over the phone from a hospital steward that a friend of mine was trying to bite holes in the detention sheet and shrieking my name.

"I grabbed a book on 'Pink Animals I Have Met' and flew to the rescue. When I got to the cot there was Edward's cherubic mug peeping out from under about four miles of nice clean bandages and an attendant sitting daintily on his chest. When he saw me he calmed down and dismissed the menagerie for the nonce. 'Dearie,' he said, taking my shrinking little hand in his, 'it was awful. It's only by mere chance that you find me custodian of this Reptile Bazar instead of one of these "mangled remains" things. It was this way. I had been down to the bar lapping up a few drinks and pretty soon a band comes up the street. I go out to look it over and there is nothing in sight, so I go back and get Arthur to mix me up another to see if it won't make me feel better. I drink that and hear the band again. I run out just in time to see it hiding behind the post. It's bum harmony at that, so I go upstairs to take a nap.

"'I'm lying there on the bed when all of a sudden the door opens and in marches twelve little soldiers, about six inches high, dressed in blue pants and red coats. They climb and start to pull off a zouave drill on the foot of the bed. That made me sour, for I don't feel like a military pageant, so I lift up my foot and kick them out on the floor. The soldiers don't say a word, but jump up and climb out through the transom. In about five minutes the door opens and in marches the whole army, all about six inches high. Gee, there must have been a million of them, for all I could see was blue pants and red coats. I'm lying there on the bed, taking it all in, when up rides a dinky little officer on a horse. He salutes me and I salute him, just to let them know that there wasn't any hard feeling. Then he says, "I am glad to state that you have but one life to lose for your country; therefore we are going to shoot you." Well, you know me, Dearie. I jumped out of the window. The next time I come out of it here is this guy doing snake charming stunts on my stomach.'

"Can you beat that for a pipe? I look after this party with all the loving care of a sister, and thanks to the doctor and a pump we pulled him through. When he was able to be shipped home I went down to the train to see him off and as he kissed me goodby he said, 'Don't you worry, kid, I won't forget this.' I didn't pay any attention to his chatter, thinking it nothing but balloon juice. But this letter says that he died about a week ago and left ten thousand to me in such a way that it won't do his wife no good to yelp. Ten thousand! Gee, ain't that an awful huge lot of money for one poor little merry-merry to be burdened with! The lawyers sent that first hundred along to show that they are not pikers, and said that the rest would be along in a few days. Gosh! I won't know what to do with it. I can't get that much in my little lisle thread bank without spoiling the contour of that new gown effect I am going to be poured into. Clothes, well I should hope so, dear. When the true meaning of that effusion soaked into my system, the way I grabbed my hat and took it on the run for the dressmaker's was a caution to cab horses.

"I'm going to get a bunch of clothes and then slide for home. You know my father was mayor of Emporia for nearly a whole term, and I can go right back into society. That is a great burg; if anybody wears anything but a Mother Hubbard on week days they are doped out as a actress. Sure! That's the way they know that there's a show in town, that and the band. That town will have nothing but the best. If a show isn't good enough to hare a band it might as well cancel. It's a great show town, all right; sometimes they have two shows there the same week, 'East Lynne' and something else. The Boston Store has the 'Pilgrim's Progress' on the recent fiction counter.

"Well, I must rush right along. I've got to go over to some place and get a mile or two of those puff gags, mine are all moth eaten. I've got some more things to buy and then I am going around and make faces at all these theatrical agents. Bye bye."

> In which Sabrina receives the balance of the fortune, says
> farewell to the hall bed-room, secures more imposing quarters, a
> French maid, an automobile and other accessories as befitting
> her station.

CHAPTER FOUR

"I've got Adversity laying on her back and purring with Contentment," remarked Sabrina the Show Girl, as she stepped out of a taxicab in front of a cafe, "and I guess she'll stand hitched for a few minutes. Tell my driver to wait and then come in and have a little liquid nourishment. This is the only place I can find where one can get any kind of service. My, ain't I getting fussy? Here 'two weeks ago coffee and butter-cakes were a banquet. But why dig up the past, and I reiterate the remark, 'Let the dead bury its dead.' If anybody mentions Mink's to me I am liable to throw a foaming fit and fall in it. Every time I pass a bread line I am filled with sorrow for the poor unfortunates, while heretofore I got sore because they had beaten me to it.

"Sure, the lawyer guy kicked in with the balance of the ten thousand, and I am now busily engaged in putting it where it will do the most good. Moved? Well, I should hope so, dear. Instead of existing in a two-by-four hallroom, with an airshaft exposure, where you have to open the door to think, I am now residing in a real suite. Maybe you think I don't keep Estelle—that's my maid—on the job. She's the busy proposition about that dump. As soon as I come out of my beauty sleep in the morning I ring the bell and in capers Estelle with a dipperful of chocolate, which I sip while reclining on my couch, and you can take it from me it's got this stunt of romping about a cold room in a canton flannel kimona trifling with the affections of a gas stove beat to a purple pulp.

"Then after reading the morning paper I arise, take a bawth, and Estelle does my hair. That is, she does part of it. I can't bear any one's teeth but my own on my Dutch braid. You know some people are sensitive that a-way. After the hair dressing number I inhale about $4 worth of breakfast and then lounge about my little nest. I call it my little nest because it is finished in birdseye maple. I always have eggs for breakfast, and Estelle puts on the finishing touches with a feather duster and I boss the job, smoking a cigarette. I always was strong for having things harmonize. I suppose it is my artistic temperament. I always drink cordials the same color as my hat. After that everything is fixed to my entire satisfaction, and I won't stand for cigarette butts being kicked under the bed, either. I'm that particular. Then about noon the dressmaker makes her entrance and I pick out my gowns. Clothes! Say, when I line out of here for that dear Emporia I'll have to buy twenty-five tickets so as I can get a baggage car free. I'll need it. From the apparel I am purchasing you'd think I was wardrobe mistress for a number two 'Talk of New York' company. If I don't make those canned goods drummers in front of the Palace Hotel think there is something in town besides a 'Tom' show I hope I never see Broadway again.

"Then along toward afternoon I climb into some chic frock—get that?—and taxey down here to look things over. Say, maybe you don't think this butterfly existence is all to the berries. The other evening I kicked down to a show I once worked in and, believe me, if some of those dames knew what they looked like from the front they certainly would rush out and hide in the cow lot.

"Honest, there is one doll who thinks she has got every prize beauty in the country biting her finger nails with jealousy. Well, she came out, led out at that. I nearly dropped dead in my seat. You know that I am not a knocker, and there is nothing I hate worse than to hear one lady pan another behind her back, so I will merely make this statement. If this person would stop trying to use up all the number 18 in the block, would get operated on for knock-knees, have her face changed and stop trying to be a very dear friend to the whole bald-headed department during the opening chorus, she'd be all right and might get a job with a medicine show. I know how she keeps her job all right, all right. I ain't mentioning any names, but a certain party, old enough to be her grandfather, had to put money into the show before they would even let her have her voice tried. I was out to dinner with the same crowd that she was with the other evening. Arthur and I were sitting at the table in the restaurant waiting for the rest of the crowd when in she canters, dressed up regardless like a queen in a book, in a low-neck gag. She run a bluff as if she just had it made, but if a certain K. & E. wardrobe mistress ever catches her with it on this party is due to get pinched for petty larceny. As soon as she spotted me she rushed over and yelped, 'Oh, Sabrina, I'm charmed to see you.' And kissed me—the cat. Then she said, 'Dearie, I understand you have inherited a fortune.' And raised her eyebrows just like that. Now I had been kidded enough about that legacy of mine, and when that doll, that ain't such a muchness herself, commences to hand out inferences, I naturally lost my goat, but remembering that I am now a lady I let go of my hatpin and merely remarked, 'Yes, but I came by it honestly, and I can safely say that I am no Foxy Grandpa's fair-haired child.'

"That terse remark made her sit up and take notice, for she had been telling one of the members of the party who she was trying to make a hit with that she got her money from her large estates in England. The only thing she knows about England she learned at a Burton Holmes lecture that she got into on a ticket she found in the subway.

"The gentlemen of the party called time and we sat down to the table. She started putting on airs and telling what she knew about the Thaw trial, so to let her know that I was right there I passed out this one, 'It's a cinch if anybody did any shooting to save your life he'll get the chair the first throw out of the box, and the jury won't be out any longer than it takes to get their hats, either.' Say, if she had had a gun she'd have shot me. One of the gentlemen remarked to me, 'You don't care for this young lady, do you?' I said, 'Sure, I like her. I like her about as much as Bingham likes Jerome.'

"This female party started to drinking champagne as if it were suds, so naturally it wasn't long before she got a snootful, and one of these crying kind, all the party began to kid her until at last she sobbed, 'Well, there is always one place I can go to where I am welcome.' One of the guys said, 'Yes, dearie, I know it, but it is after 1 o'clock now and that place is closed.' Then little Bright Eyes beat it and we all had a real nice evening after that. Oh! She's a smooth one, all right; she nearly made me lose my job once if it hadn't been that the stage manager was carrying my suitcase I would have been decorated with my little two weeks out in the wilds somewhere. You see it was this way: We had a tree, not the one Arthur owned, but another, and one of the comedians had to stand inside of it for about fifteen minutes before he could make his entrance—laughing number—this was only a dinky little place and only had one small airhole. Well, this foxy dame stuffed this airhole full of limberger cheese, so when it came time for his entrance instead of coming forth blithe and gay as per book, the comedian came out looking as if he had apoplexy, the same naturally causing the merry-merry to giggle ad lib. Did you ever see a wild fish? Honest, when that man came off I thought he was going to commit murder; what he said on the subject is not for me to repeat. Right in the middle of the harangue this dame remarks, 'I think it was Sabrina.'

"The next think she thunk was to wonder who let go of the asbestos curtain, for I happened to overhear that 'aside' and bounced a stage-brace on her think tank. If she had gone on again that night it would have been in a wheeled chair. Another stunt she did was to put lampblack all over the tenor's glove and he wiped it off on the prima's shoulders so she looked like a zebra in a bathing suit, and every time she would tell the firemen when the chorus men were getting fresh courage by smoking cigarettes in their dressing rooms, but that is all over now and my stage career is ended until I spend all this surplus cash. I take it on the run for that dear Kansas tomorrow, so I think I will go and see if Estelle has finished packing. Try and be good while I am gone, and if anything happens for goodness sake wire me, for out in that neck of the woods even paying for telegrams from New York is a pleasure. Au revoir."

In which Sabrina makes a visit to her parents in Emporia, returns after but a brief stay and chronicles some of the events that transpired while in the city of her birth.

CHAPTER FIVE

"Kill the prodigal, the calf has returned!" cried Sabrina the Show Girl, as her taxicab drew up to where we were standing.

"Thought you were in Emporia!" we exclaimed in surprise.

"I was. I came; I saw; I conquered. Or whatever whoever said it, did. Jump in and I'll tell you all about it. Fine business. I had more exciting events than ever appeared before under one canvas. But never again. You know when I started about ten days ago? Trouble? Why, I had more trouble than a manager with nine stars and one good dressing room. And I had to leave Estelle, my maid, here at that. I tried to get a stateroom, but nothing doing, so me for a berth with the common herd. Train going along fine, about 3 in the morning me pounding my fair young ear in lower six, when all of a sudden. Biff! Mr. Engine slaps a cow in the back and the whole works deserts the track and the caboose I'm in slides over the bank, turns over on her side and dies, lower six at the bottom. I get handed the following—one suitcase, two pairs of shoes and a fat hardware salesman from upper five. Not forgetting my womanly rights I turn loose a rebel yell and start to climb out of the opposite window with the kind assistance of the arm of the berth, the face of the fat salesman and a broken window, appearing as the Pink Pajama Girl on the side of the car that was at that time understudying the roof.

"When I got out I turned loose a couple more whoops on the clear morning air just to let them know that I was still on the job, and took a casual survey of the disaster. Naturally our car was the goat and the only one that had gone wrong. The fat salesman does the appearing act next, dragging his suitcase; waived formality and asked me if I would have a drink. Me for the drink, and then I got him to climb back down and rescue the rest of my apparel, and I dressed standing up there on the side of the car, much to the edification of the train crew that were not busily engaged in assuring the other dames in the car that they were not dead. By and by along comes another train, and they load us all in and we get to Chicago only about four hours late. Me being that fatigued I rushed right up to the Sherman House, but there wasn't a room vacant on the top floor, so I knew I would not feel at home there, so I go capering over to the Annex.

"Gee, but that Chicago is a bum town, and yet in Emporia they look upon it as a Mecca of pleasure. The only pleasure I ever got there was trying to analyze the smells from the stock yards. They don't eat anything in Chicago but chop suey. Did you ever shoot any of that junk into your system? Them can have it that likes it; but never again for muh. You get it in a little dish, and the blooming stuff smells as if it was some relation to a poultice; you eat it and then go home and chew all the enamel off the bed. No, I don't know what it is made of; if I did I wouldn't eat it. That's the only thing Chicago is good for, chop suey and smells. When they get through talking about the World's Fair perhaps they will think up some new form of amusement. I met a wop in Chicago, one of these real romantic kind that only grow there. I was seated in a secluded corner of the ladies' waiting room of the Annex, and he came up and asked me if I didn't want to step in the Pompeian room and hear the waters of the fountain lapping up against the marble. I told him I much preferred to be up against a bottle of wine and do the lapping myself. He, with that true Chicago gallantry, said, 'Excuse me first, I want to 'phone a friend.'

"I'm glad I didn't hold my breath while he was gone. I think he must have taken a surface car for Oak Park. Those Chicago rum-dums are the true sports, all right, all right. If necessity compels them to buy anything stronger than beer they commence to look sassy at the waiter and talk loud. Chicago is sure rightly named when they call it the Windy City. You just ought to have heard the line of jolly some of those boys tried to hand out to me. To me, mind you, to me! They must have thought that I was some unsophisticated young ingenue that never had been further away from State street than an occasional excursion across the lake to St. Joe.

"I sloshed around town for a couple of days just to give those people a change from the usual run of Randolph street romps, then I hit the hummer for bleeding Kansas and Emporia.

"Say, I had a great first entrance into that burg and nothing else; but a crate of lemons got off to crab the act. When I climb down off the hurdle, behold, the village choir right there on the job to see the train come in. The arrival of the train—notice the train—is what you might call the main event of the day. As soon as the village yokels saw my trunks being unloaded they all did the grand duck for the theatre to strike the house manager, thinking it was a show. I hadn't tipped my mitt to the folks, so they were not at the tank to give me the parental embrace, but after giving the necessary instructions to the baggage man I climbed into the Palace Hotel bus and romped up to my ancestors' abode.

"Business of weeping on neck. Mother wigwags father, who comes over from the grocery store, where he is electing the President of the United States. Business of rejoicing ad. lib. Sister comes in from the village school; neighbors kick in to see what's coming off. Entrance of trunks, gasps of surprise by populace. Distribution of presents by muh.

"That night there was a young people's meeting at the church. A young people's meeting is a signal for every old dame in the township that's not married to iron out her white silk waist and take it on the run for the tabernacle. After the usual prelude the minister got up and said, 'We would like a few words from Sabrina, who has lately returned to our little flock from the busy scenes of the great and wicked metropolis.' I had to get up and hand out the usual stereotyped and mimeographed stuff about being glad to be in their midst once again and it did my heart good to see so many bright and shining faces, etc., etc. I had on a modest little frock that had only lanced me about three hundred and made the aurora borallis look like a dark night. So that the admiring public wouldn't overlook any bets in the costume line I enlivened my discourse with these illustrated song gestures, every move a picture.

"After the olio the Busy Brigade of the Ladies' Auxiliary took the napkin off a group of sandwiches and a bath tub of lemonade and we all had an awful time with ourselves cracking rare quips. Me the center of an admiring throng. They all knew I was an actress and they asked me to act. You know the extent of my acting, a champagne dance and a burlesque on the 'Merry Widow' waltz, and my lines are limited to, 'Oh! girls, here comes the prince, now, hurrah, hurrah, hurrah.' Therefore I ducked the request to exhibit my art. I was going home after the show—I mean entertainment—and Waldo, the fellow I went with before I got sense enough to blow the burg with a musical comedy—Waldo started to walk home with me. I will say this much for Waldo before I go any further, he has a good eye for the future, even though he is working in a grocery store.

"Waldo and I were walking down the quiet country lane, he telling me all the news that had been pulled off while I had been away. When we got down to the garden gate what do you think came off? Waldo proposed. Honest, he proposed, just like that. Waldo's intentions were sincere, but his work was lumpy and he went up in his lines a couple of times. He didn't pass it out half as strong as these city chaps do when they don't mean it. I instructed Waldo to can his chatter and forget it. Waldo got real indignant because I wouldn't fly with him and tried to grab me. Now I hadn't been prowling about New York alone without learning how to take care of myself, so I gave him the heel and the way he went to the mat was a caution for further orders. Waldo was a nice boy, but he was rough, so after the jolt he got he had sense enough to beat it.

"Say, I had an awful time for the next two or three days. But never again. I'll never go any further out in the country than Claremont. These rural districts are for those that like them, but if I can have Broadway for a country lane you won't hear a peep out of me. Honest, when I see a car with 'Forty-second street, crosstown,' on it I wanted to gallup up and kiss the motorman.

"Well, I've got to leave you here. Will tell you how I happened to leave Emporia the next time I see you. Take it from me, I had rather be a shine on Broadway than a glare anywhere else. So long."

In which Sabrina chronicles some more of the adventures that happened to her while visiting her parents and details how she stood the town on edge, was ejected therefrom, and the remarks she made on the subject.

CHAPTER SIX

"They say a rolling stone gathers no moss, but it's a cinch that this pebble could have gathered a bunch of lemons since she has fallen into her inheritance if she had but listened to their plaintive plea," remarked Sabrina, the Show Girl, after we had seated ourselves at the table.

"Has some one been seeking your hand in marriage?" she was asked.

"Honest, there are more dubs around this town who had rather get married than work than there are actors on Broadway now. I have had three proposals since I have been back, one of marriage. I told them all 'no.' That I preferred to live a la carte. I could have become a farmer's bride in Emporia if I had but said the word. I didn't tell you how I came to sneak that snare, did I? You know I went out there with the intention of staying a month, surging around and showing the village belles that May Manton wasn't the only authority on correct dress. Ten days was my limit.

"The family and every one agreed that my metropolitan broadmindedness was too much of a strain on the sense of morality of the peasantry, as it were. No, nothing of the slightest consequence, nothing that would have caused the inhabitants of Broadway to even arch their eyebrows. All I did was to inhale a snootful and go out with a friend and stand the thriving little village of Emporia up on end and tip it over. 'Tis a strange tale. List, and I will unfold it to you. One day I was wafting slowly and sedately down to the Boston Store for my mail when lo! and behold, what did I see out in front of the Palace Hotel but an automobile. Believe me when I tell you, it was the first time I had looked a radiator in the face for a week. Two young fellows were monkeying around the machine, and as they were nice-looking chaps I gave them the furtive glance, and one of them stopped and asked me if he hadn't been introduced to me in the Harlem Casino. At any other time I would have taken his remark as a deep insult, inferring as it did that I was so far from Forty-second street, but now I could have fell on his neck and cried with joy. I told him that I had never met him in the place he had mentioned, but to let it go at that, and if he even knew where Harlem was it was introduction enough.

"Come to find out they were making a trip across the continent, and had stopped there to get a little gasolene for the machine. We talked things over and I found out that they knew several people I did, and anyway they were from New York and that helped a heap. They were going to leave that afternoon, but I prevailed upon them to stay over until the next day. I was invited into the hotel for dinner, and we opened the first bottle of champagne wine, as they say out West, that had been opened in Emporia since the Governor went through. In truth, the bottle was covered with specks, and the label had faded so you could hardly read it, but when the cork went 'wop!' three traveling men at the next table burst into tears.

"After we had consumed all the champagne wine they had in the snare, I tipped them off to a speak-easy, and we decided to ride down there in the machine, and then go for a little tour, as it were. By this time it had been noised through the city that some one had taken the bottle out of the show window, and a large crowd had assembled to see the plutocrats come forth. We capered blithely out to the machine, climbed in and hiked for the blind tiger. After the usual red tape the captain sold us about two quarts of jig-juice—the kind that makes a jack-rabbit spit in a bulldog's eye.

"Anon, we again went for a ride, and I am here to state that the way we breezed through that village made the proverbial Kansas cyclone look as if it was running on crutches. The inhabitants that didn't duck for the cellars stood on the plankwalk and made rude and discomplimentary remarks. Some well-meaning Rube had tipped his mitt to the town marshal, and that worthy cluck had stretched a rope from the blacksmith shop to the corner of the livery stable, so naturally we had to pause. Enter Marshal R.U.E. with business of making a pinch. After filing the usual protests we were haled before the Magistrate. Here's a copy of the testimony:

Marshal—Judge, Your Honor, these prisoners are charged with defacing landmarks, violating the pure food law, exceeding the speed limit and disorderly conduct. Judge, Your Honor, these miscreants defaced our landmarks by drinking the only bottle of champagne wine that has ever been in our village—the bottle that for so long has graced the window of our leading hotel and was looked on with pride and reverence by the townspeople. A bottle that has been cherished for generations until these monsters came with their ill-gotten gold and purchased same.

They violated the pure food law by drinking said bottle of champagne which has been proven by the State Board of Examiners to contain 18 per cent. alcohol. The aforesaid prisoners exceeded the speed limit by rushing through our quiet streets at a terrific pace, to the danger of the lives and limbs of our wives and children.

The prisoners at the bar are charged with disorderly conduct by the following facts: They emptied said bottle of champagne, which was reputed to hold one quart. That bottle of said wine was emptied completely, which is proven by your marshal, who, after the orgy in our leading hotel, did approach a waiter of said hotel and ask for a taste of said wine, but upon investigation the bottle was found to be entirely empty.

The aforesaid bottle contained one whole quart of an intoxicating beverage and was distributed among three people. Therefore, Judge, Your Honor, the prisoners must have been intoxicated and therefore disorderly. Your Honor, the prosecution rests its case.

Judge—Prisoners, step to the bar. You are charged with, etc., ad lib. What have you to say before sentence is passed upon you?

Prisoners—Not a blamed word.

Judge—I find the prisoners guilty and sentence them to pay a fine of $50, or ten days in the city prison.

Prisoners—Gee, you must be going to build a new courthouse.

Judge—Five dollars for kidding the court.

"I knew those fellows couldn't stand the strain of the $55 fine, so, turning my back in maidenly modesty to the court, I dug down in the lisle-thread bank and came up with a hundred dollar bill, the first one ever seen in Emporia. I tossed it carelessly on the desk, remarking, 'Take it out of that.' You could have knocked the court's eyes off with a club. I don't think he ever saw that much money in one group before in his life. The clerk of the court grabbed the fresh-air fund and did a rubber into the family safe for the change. All quiet along the Potomac. The whole blooming city didn't have change for a century note. Can you beat that? And they say there is no graft in Kansas. They had to go over to the speakeasy for a change. What do you know about that? A court of a Prohibition State going to a gin-mill for money.

"After we got through telling the court what he reminded us of and what he looked like, we tripped out to the machine and climbed on board and started out again. We rode around until 3 or 4 o'clock in the morning, and I got to bed just as the help was getting out to do the chores. Maybe you don't think that evening's amusement caused some scandal.

"Why, before breakfast the entire population was wise to the fact that Sabrina, the pride and glory of the village, was out drinking liquor and playing progressive hell with a couple of strange gentlemen.

"If you want anything known in one of those wopburgs, just tell it to the butcher—it's got a town crier or a litho threesheet faded. Mother had the info on the whole game before she got the curl papers out of her hair. A couple of the Ladies' Auxiliary to the Herbert Killjoy Memorial did picket duty out in front of the house all night so as to be first in with the glad tidings.

"They galloped up like Sheridan twenty miles away. The Killjoy sisters beat it, and I was just assuring mother that getting pinched was considered very distingue by the upper crust of the eastern metropolis when in prance the village selectmen followed by the deacons of the church. When they came into view I knew the bell had rung on Sabrina, the souse. They all came in looking like the first act of a funeral, and Homer Jenkins, the head deaconorine, looked real solemn, and said, 'We regret to inform you that we have found it our painful duty to dismiss your daughter from the church.' I spoke up real gay like and said, 'Go as far as you like, I never was a commuter anyway.'

"The selectmen were at the bat next and the main guy of that informed father that I would have to be put under bond to keep the peace, as my actions of yesterday in drinking the champagne wine had caused nine of the village near-sports to get stewed on Rhinewine and seltzer, and to please let them have the money now, as they had to pay the mayor's salary to-morrow. Then I delivered my philippic as follows: 'If you spangled-eyed dubs think you are going to shake me down for any more change you had better drop in your penny and get next to yourselves. Nix, not. I've already coughed up more than the rest of the entire population, and you are not going to lance me for any more just because I've got a bundle. You're good people, you've got big feet, and I would like to see you run fast. Now beat it. I'm going to blow the burg on the next caboose, and while I don't wish you any bad luck I hope the town hall burns down. Now take it on the run or I will give you all a good scolding and send you to bed.' And the funny thing about it is, they slid. I tell the folks that my light is hid under a bushel in Emporia, grab the bus, and here I am and nothing short of an explosion will make me leave. Put this on your 'call board,' the only good thing about these hick hamlets is they remind you of New York because they are so different. So long. Don't fall down the elevator shaft."

In which Sabrina attends a ball given by the Chorus Girls' Union and frivols extensively in the vineyard and later does a specialty with ice skates and a bottle of arnica.

CHAPTER SEVEN

"All work and no play makes Jack a dead one," remarked Sabrina, the Show Girl, as we met her at the appointed place. "Don't I look like the wreck of the Hesperus? Honest to goodness, I feel like nine dollars' worth of dog meat hanging out of a hospital window. Was you at the ball, also? I mean did you attend last night's festivities? Ah, me! The joy and laughter of yesterday is sure the hangover of today. I thought I would caper down to the ball last night and just see how the other half lived, and instead of being a mere obtrusive observer I developed into what you might term the main event of the evening. You see it was this way. The Chorus Girls' Union, of which I am now a member, gave a ball in commemoration of the event of the Mayor vetoing Tim Sullivan's bill about women smoking in public. It was instigated by the 'Knight for a Day' girls, because when they went to plead before the Aldermen the newspapers forgot to mention the show they were from, so that the long talk didn't do the press agent any material good, as it were. The hall was tastily decorated with pictures of the Aldermen embellished with cigarette butts and champagne corks.

"By the way, if you see smoke coming from the Knickerbocker Theatre Building, don't turn in a fire alarm, for it is just the Friars showing their good feeling by trying to smoke up all the Friar cigars and cigarettes in town.

"All of our set was there, and numerous telegrams of regret were read from the road companies. As I say, I was seated quietly in a rathskeller listening to the noise, when one of the young ladies inadvertently remarked that there was to be big doings at a nearby hall, and suggested that as she was selling tickets, it would be a good plan to buy some and go and look the affair over, not to mingle with the throng, but merely to add tone to the event. That listened very well indeed, and we all climbed into a cabbage and vamped over.

"We managed to secure a box and were seated surveying the dancers, of which there were a few, and the wine agents, of which there was a herd, until one of the said agents happened to spy our little crowd, and with that true Southern gallantry for which wine agents are so noted, he sent over a quart bottle for each one of the party, but in the excitement of the moment forgot to include glasses, so rather than look a gift horse in the mouth, metaphorically speaking, we did not mention the oversight and contented ourselves with drinking out of the bottles in true democratic spirit. Did you ever imbibe Tiffany Water direct from its native heath, as it were? No? Then let me warn you from that lurking pitfall. It has the same taste, but the effect, di mi, the effect is multiplied by six.

"All of a sudden I became inoculated with a wild desire to burst forth into song, and also with the idea that when it came to tripping the light fantastic toe I had Genee looking like the first lesson in a $5 course. With that hunch in mind I shook the rest of the mob and descended to the floor accompanied by my personal press agent. I was wearing, at the time, one of my latest importations both underneath and outside. When the band for the nineteenth time struck up the 'Merry Widow' waltz, by permission of Henry W. Savage, I capered out upon the floor, where, much to the edification of the assembled multitude, I pulled off a combination of the 'Merry Widow' waltz and Dance of the Seven Veils that will be the talk of the town until Bingham does something else foolish. Did it cause excitement! Well, say, if it hadn't been for the kindness of a friend I would at this time been pacing a prison corridor in striped pajamas.

"Honest, when I came to this morning and Estelle—that's my maid—told me what I had done, I vowed that I never would speak to a wine agent again, for I was just that mortified. After me remembering to be a lady, and then before a mob to kick over the traces and crab the act. Believe me, every time I see an advertisement for that brand of wine a blush mantles my cheeks. Sure, I can blush. See. And for tears, it's just like turning on the faucet in the bath tub. All the young creatures in our set have to be there with the blush of modesty and the tear tank, for in the heat and gayety of a wine party, when some one springs a travelling man's story if we couldn't flash a flush we would be doped out as being brazen hussies, and tears are always handy. Either for the police, the landlord or an ardent suitor. The modern girl has to be equipped for any emergency like a hook and ladder truck. But here I am giving away all our girlish secrets.

"Take it from me I'll never again gallop around the juniper bowl. I wouldn't be a lush worker like that Alla McCune for another $10,000 legacy. She's just started the habit lately. She thinks it's stylish. Sure, every time she goes out with a crowd that drink anything stronger than beer she thinks she is in society. Every time she gets a snoot full she falls in love. Fact. My, such a scene as she caused in the hotel the other evening. She doped it out this way: She was all alone, a stormy night, a bottle of Scotch and a syphon. Why not light up? Talk about your Great White Way, why, she had it looking like a dark alley in Darkest Brooklyn. Along about 6 o'clock in the evening a gentleman called to see her. As soon as he entered the portal Alla knew that she had at last met her soul twin.

"She was hanging on to the table at the time and when she let go to embrace him, instead of being clasped to his yearning bosom, as she had planned, her knees gave away and she skated on her profile across the divan. This cluck, being of a timid nature, instead of running for the ammonia, slammed the door and sprinted for the elevator. Alla, as soon as the door closed, realized that she had been jilted, and resolving not to be canned without a struggle, she threw on her pony coat over her kimono, and pinning her hat roguishly over one ear, she fled the snare and ran down eight flights of steps into the street, with two coon bell boys after her. She turned into Broadway, going like Hose No. 7, with her kimono streaming to the breeze, and ran all the way down to Rector's and into the door before she was stopped by the head waiter. The two bell boys caught up and loaded her into a cab before the police came and managed to get her back up to the hotel, though the fight she put up was a caution. Wine is sure a mocker and Scotch highballs is fierce.

"I heard from the folks in Emporia the other day and they are still talking over the time I and the two guys in the automobile pulled off. The minister sprung a long sermon on the effects of strong drink on the young and the Emporia Wasp—you know they did call it the Bee, but the guy that bought it from the Bee people renamed it the Wasp, because he got stung worse than any bee could sting—the Emporia Wasp came out with a long editorial about the profligate rich and the Attic Debating Society had a big pow-wow in the basement of the church on the subject, 'Be it Resolved, That more people are killed by strong drink than by hanging.' All this had such a moral effect on the young that the soda fountain didn't sell a claret phosphate for three weeks after. And the Ladies' Aid got so busy over Azbe Lewis, the town drunkard, that he had three proposals of marriage, but he decided to take the lesser of the evils and stick to drink. I think he ain't such a dope at that.

"Say, sniff. Can you detect the low, plaintive cry of an arnica bottle? I am learning how to skate. Yes, I fell for it. Fell for it is good. 'Course I did. All over the ice. You see it was this way. I was up to a tea one of the girls gave in honor of the judge getting a divorce from his wife—we call it a tea because there wasn't any there. We were all sitting around panning those who were not among those present, until at last one of the girls who didn't dare leave till the party broke up suggested that we go down to the park and take a skate. The hostess was real nice. She suggested that it wasn't necessary to beat it clear down there to get a skate, as she had some in the house, and if we drank that up the Dutchman on the corner knew she was good for any amount within reason. But we didn't mean what she meant, so we departed. Going down I became perhaps a little too excited over the coming event and went to some length to inform the assembled skirts that when it came to cutting ice I, not seeking to boast, but I was there, forte, and such pastimes as writing names or doing Dutch rolls I considered rudimentary in the skating number and only performed by the immature.

"I may have overestimated my ability some, for I had never been on skates before in my life, but I'm no piker and I follow that old principle of willing to try anything once, so when it came time I let the boy put the skates on without a murmur, and was assisted to the ice by about six or eight eager hands. Say, I looked out at the gang gliding about, gave the signal to let go the ropes and took the fatal step. Curtain. Say, I went round so fast both skates clinched in my marcel wave. Would you believe it, there wasn't hardly any one in sight when I started falling, but before I got through the police had to move the crowd on. The only thing I could do gracefully was to throw a faint. I turned one loose until somebody tried to force a glass between my teeth and then I came to, but it was only water, so I had a relapse. Then a nice gent kicked in with a flask and I came to. Maybe you think those artful kidders didn't hand it to me. Anybody but a lady would have lost her temper and cursed them. But I told them where to get off, and don't you forget it, but I used no language that would have led people to think I was anything but what I should be. After that I managed to skate around a little, but let me tell you, that night I got down on the floor to take my shoes off all right, but it took Estelle—that's my maid—and a derrick to get me up again. Say, it's getting late and I must be going. You know Mabel is now a bride again, and her little husband has been staying down at the club instead of loitering about the flat, so the other night when he knocked on the door to get in, Mabel said, 'Is that you, Charles?' And now she can't get him out of the house nights. You see, her husband's name is Arthur. So long."

Sabrina now falls in love with a press agent with the hectic chatter. He proposes and is accepted, and Sabrina shows her love and devotion by going his bail when he is arrested for permitting his jealousy to get the better of him in a restaurant.

CHAPTER EIGHT

Who's the guy that said "Love laughs at locksmiths?" Just show him to muh. I'll show him where he got in wrong. It's enough to get a perfect lady's goat. My Wilbur tried it the night he got pinched, and all he got was a clout on the knob from the desk sergeant and a languishing number in a prison, and I don't dare to go within a mile of the drum.

The way I caper from one tribulation to another would make a sick woman out of far stronger than me. Yes, I have at last found a man that loves me for myself alone. He's a press agent, and he hands it out so sincere that I know he must mean part of it. He's going to buy me an engagement ring as soon as he gets his expense account. He's with a Broadway musical comedy, and though he has run some of the girls' pictures, he has not made the slightest advance toward any of them.

He's been coming to see me for nearly a month. My heart went out to him the minute he said he had a stand in with three city editors.

Us actresses never get over our theatrical training. He's a quiet party, and instead of hanging about the Knickerbocker bar with the rest of the agents, he stays in the office and pounds out copy. He gave me a beautiful silk parasol that I know didn't cost him less than four pairs of seats. And all this before he asked me for my hand in marriage.

Honest, I'll never forget the night he proposed as long as I live. Not that I never was proposed to before, and some of them would have had me starred, but the romantic surroundings and all that kind of thing. It was this way: Me and him were the guests at a beefsteak party, and after the fourth drink he commenced to show me marked attention, and when we got out of the cab in front of my hotel he offered to help me upstairs, though I generally have a bellboy for that purpose, and when we had got up in my apartment and Estelle had gone to give the bellhop a quarter and the pitcher, he popped the question, and such beautiful language, I remembered it the next morning and wrote it down.

He held my shrinking little hand in his and said, "Say, Kid, you've made an awful good showing with me. Believe it, I could plant your stuff all the rest of my life, and while I ain't much of a litho myself, still I can get away with it and am the man who invented red on yellow. I can't pay for many electric signs for you, but still if you'll plant your heart in my cut-trunk I'll guarantee there won't be any excess and I'm making money enough to O.K. most of your extras.

"Listen, Party, we'll split my salary fifty-fifty every Saturday night. I got good backing in the bank, and I want you to be my little star. You angel!"

Wasn't that sweet? That word angel aroused my suspicions for the nonce, for angels are the ones who generally get lanced, but he handed it out so fervent that I knew he would make good on some of the points, so from force of habit I said, "Bring out your contract."

And with those tender words and the pitcher the bellhop had brought back we plighted our troth.

What do you know about that? I don't believe I ever before was as much in love as I am now. Why, I ain't been to see any other show but his for two weeks. Of course, I have been engaged before and handed out this eye-glistening-with-adoration gag before, but it was done only to vary the monotony of my former theatrical career and increase my income.

What! Sure I get an allowance from the fellows I'm engaged to. It's only fair. Ain't I got a trooso to buy? Te, he!

If I'd saved all the money I have been given to purchase troosos with I would have a bunch that would make Gladys Vanderbilt's layout look like a gingham wrapper. Sure, ain't it worth money to those wops to have the pure love of a good, true girl? Gee, don't make me laugh like a baby.

I was betrothed to six at one time, and the diamond rings I wore made the prima bite her finger-nails with jealousy. Oh, I had a great graft.

I had a birthday in every week stand. System? Well, I should hope so, dear.

We'd work it this way: Alla McSweeney and I were chumming together, and naturally Monday night after the show we would meet some folks. We would have a real nice time, and along about fourth highball time after the show Wednesday night Alla would whisper real confidential into one of the fellows' ear that I was going to be twenty-one Friday and "we girls" are planning to give her a little surprise, and did he want to come in on it.

Every time the Johns would fall, except in Milwaukee, and nobody ever got anything out of that town anyway. Then Alla would whisper that the company was going to present me with a loving cup because I was such a good fellow, and if they wanted to chip in now was their chance, and anything was acceptable from $5 up, and to bring his friends.

Alla would tout it up something fierce, I being totally unconscious to what was coming off.

Friday night would come around and Alla would borrow the loving cup from the property man that the tenor used in the drinking number, put it under her shawl and caper over to the appointed cafe.

I would be the center of a bunch of merry cut-ups all wanting to blow out the candles on my birthday cake.

After the wine got to flowing freely and the crowd all jolly Alla would drag out the prop and make a nice little speech on behalf of the company.

Me—you know I would be that flustered that I didn't know what to do, and when Alla would say that other people beside the members of the company had assisted I would be so gratified that I could scarce keep back the tears.

All the clucks that hadn't chipped in would feel so bad because they weren't included in my outburst of gratitude that nine times out of ten they would sneak out and try to break into a jewelry store.

Then Saturday Alla and I would do the great divide.

Take it from me, when I came in off the road that season I had a roll of the evergreen that looked like a bundle of hall carpet.

But now that I am an heiress I do not have to adopt those subterfuges in order to get the daily Java. But I couldn't work those stunts on my Wilbur; he's too wise, and being in the business he's hep to all that kind of work.

He's a good, nice, honest fellow, as press agents go, and I think I can safely trust him with my innocent heart.

If he don't—well, you know me. If he don't think he run up against the business end of a cyclone it will be because I got throat trouble and can't talk.

Honest, my fair young brow is commencing to get wrinkled trying to dope out whether I want to become a bride or lead the free and easy life of a bachelor girl.

Of course, if I get married and don't like it divorces are easy enough to get, and then being a widow saves a girl a whole lot of embarrassment, for she don't have to pretend to not understand some of the innuendoes that are now and then sprung during the modern conversations.

But, on the other hand, Wilbur isn't there with a very big fresh air fund, and by perseverance I might cop out a Pittsburg millionaire and become famous.

Marriage is worse than a lottery; it's a strong second for the show business. You never can tell.

Wilbur sure does treat me nice—he's promised that I shall be a flower girl at the Friar Festival when it comes off in May. Ain't that nice of him?

Gee, but that's going to be the grand doings.

Are you going to the ball?

Say, the round of festivities I am pulling off lately would make a person think I was a society bud.

Oh, come closer, listen. A certain party wants me to go out in vaudeville. What do you know about that? Can you see me doing two-a-day and getting in a contest with Eva Tanguay or Vesta Victoria or the Russell Brothers. I would go in a minute, though I promised mother when I quit burlesque that I would never again wear tights.

When I was in the business if I couldn't get a job on my voice all I had to do was to flash a photo taken as Captain of the High Jinks Cadets, and then—in a minute.

Flo. Ziegfield made me all kinds of offers to go in the "Soul Kiss," but the blondes were all full, and you can see me in a brindle wig?

I am willing to sacrifice nearly anything for Art, but when it comes to leaving nineteen dollars' worth of puffs in a dressing room where you can't pick your company, not for little Sabrina.

I used to have trouble enough with my number eighteen and lip stick and the bunch of near-lady kleptomaniacs that the manager made a great mistake taking on the road in the last show I was with.

Well, to get back to vaudeville, I don't know whether to do a single turn or put on a big act with a dancing scene or a prizefight in it. Those things go big nowadays.

I could get the music publishers to slip me a little on the side for using their songs, too. Of course I don't need the money, for I've got the biggest part of that ten thou. inheritance left yet; but still it would keep me busy and away from the cafes, for now all I do all day long is to roam around from one place to another imbibing booze and balloon juice.

It's beautiful billiards all right for the time being, but I always feel so on the blink the next morning.

Wilbur doesn't care; that is, he said he knew I had artistic temperament, and if I wanted to get it out of my system, vaudeville was as good as anything.

I was talking to a guy the other day that is in vaudeville, and he said that down around the St. James Building you could buy acts by the pound.

Another guy wanted to take my money and star me in a musical comedy. Wasn't he the kind gent?

Gee, I didn't tell you how Wilbur come to get pinched, did I? Well, it was this way:

You know Wilbur is of Spanish descent even though he was born in Canarsie, and he has a very jealous disposition; so the night after I had promised to be his own little star of hope he discovered me in a certain cafe with another party. This other party was a dramatic critic and I was touting Wilbur's show, but Wilbur didn't know that, so when he saw me sitting there having the time of my young life he lost his nanny and caused a scene, forgetting this other party was a critic in his passion.

The head waiter threw them both out, and the critic, seeing the police coming, said: "This is an actor trying to lick me," and naturally the cops nearly beat poor Wilbur to a pulp.

I went down to the station house and tried to get Wilbur out, but the police were so rude that I had to tell them where to get off, and they threatened to jug me, so I slid.

Wilbur got out the next day, though, and told me over the 'phone that he loved me all the more for trying to come to his rescue. I wish they would import the Emporia police force here. I can lick him myself.

My! is it that late? Wilbur will be waiting to take me over to Childs'. So long!

Sabrina returns to the chorus so that she can keep an apartment, a maid and an automobile without causing comment. She also talks of getting a house-boat for the summer with some girl friends and discourses on the advisability of having the wardrobe mistress for a chaperone.

CHAPTER NINE

"Virtue has its own reward and that's all it ever gets," remarked Sabrina, the Show Girl, as we met her on the street. "I am once again a wage-earner. This floating around town as one of the idle rich is all to the peaches for a while, but as a continuous performance it makes a poor showing. You know when I first became an heiress I had a call-board put up in my boudoir and a little notice pinned on it that read, 'Rehearsal, 10 o'clock to-morrow, everybody,' and then I would lay in bed all morning and make faces at it.

"Everybody had a large bunch of fun kidding me about my inheritance till I was nearly bug. Why, would you believe it? I couldn't go to dinner or riding with a gentleman friend, but some humorous dame sitting at another table would arch her eyebrows and then, if I introduced them to the gent, they would say, 'I am very glad to meet you, Mr. Suchandsuch; how are things in Pittsburg?'

"At last it got so bad that I decided to go back to work and earn my little twenty per, so that I could keep my automobile and wear good clothes without the slightest taint of suspicion on my character. With that noble end in view I started on the still hunt. Nothing doing with that traveling thing.

"I tucked my little scrapbook under my arm and sat in the waiting-room. After hanging around in there for about half an hour I would be permitted to glide into the big boss. I had a nice little monologue framed up as to my virtues—no, that's the wrong word—ability.

"None of the managers asked me what I had done, but what did I GET.

"When I called on the gentlemen by whom I am now employed he said: 'Talent? Oh, piffle! Can you wear tights?' He said that to me.

"I merely mentioned that I used to work for Mr. Ziegfeld and he hired me at once. I didn't even have to show him my picture taken as Aphrodite in a classical art study.

"I went over to rehearsal, and of all the frowsy dames I ever piped—far be it from me to knock, but they looked like a bunch of pie-trammers that had just rushed over from Child's. The stage manager was a friend of mine, and I asked him when he had started an old ladies' home, and he told me—mind you, this is the strictest confidence—that the divorce courts and the cheap rates from Pittsburg was raising Cain with the crop of merry-merries.

"I was standing over near the piano when the leading lady galloped in. Believe me the dog she put on would make you think that she had every other star looking like a twinkle, and before she landed where she is now she was leading lady for a moving picture company.

"But the comedian—honest, when he gets a couple under his belt he is just that funny—gee! I nearly howled my head off at him calling the tenor Gertrude.

"Say, he got awfully peevish and was mad enough to crush a grape when he found out that he couldn't have the 'spot' when he does his duet number with the ingenue, and when he found out that he would have to dress with the character comedian, who is a low, coarse brute, always drinking beer in the dressing room and not sharing with anybody, he got so mad I thought he would burst into tears.

"He's another of these exaggerated ego guys, every move a picture, wears his handkerchief up his sleeve and all that kind of guff.

"The funniest thing about the whole show is that the author is staging the piece, and what he don't know about the show business would make the Lenox Library look like a news stand He wanted the tenor to hold the prima so she couldn't show her rings. And that's the only thing that got her the job—her jewelry.

"We open in Hartford in a couple of weeks and then play Washington and then come in here for a run.

"Honest, the way those two towns fall for this: 'Manager Soandso is to be congratulated upon securing for his next week's attraction Mr. Suchandsuch's elaborate production of the great London success, 'The Rancid Prune,' with the following all-star cast of metropolitan favorites.' And some of them, ach, Himmel!

"I do wish that the merry Springtime would hurry up and kick in. Them can have the Winter that likes it, but not for little Angel-face; give me the summer and that 'Robins Nest Again' number.

"When the bock beer signs again wave in the breeze and the Dutchman in the delicatessen don't think you are a bug when you ask for Summer sausage; when the mint commences to sprout in the cigar box on the fire escape and all nature seems glad. I just love those trips on the night boat up the Hudson with the searchlight: shining on the trees and the ice tinkling in the highball glass as the steward comes down the deck.

"You know that I am naturally—even when sober—of a romantic and emotional temperament, but those nights I can sit and hold hands and inhale cocktails until daylight without an effort.

"And then Sundays down at Manhattan Beach dubbing around in a bathing suit—and take this from me as advance information, the bathing suit I am going to wear this year is going to chase the waves clear out in the ocean. I don't know yet whether I can wear it at Rockaway or not; it's a cinch I can't if they have another moral wave like they did last year. It's chic without being bizarre.

"And I can safely say without fear of successful contradiction that I look well in it, and if I can keep my hair from getting wet I'll be the one best bet. But if the briny mingles with my marcel wave—good night, nurse!

"One of Mr. Hepner's assistants told me that if salt water ever touched my golden tresses that the only thing I could do to keep them from turning green was to get scalped.

"A friend of mine who owns a yacht is going to send his wife and daughter on a trip to Europe, and he told me to count myself one of a party of six that are going to make a tour of all the neighboring resorts—no, not that kind— Summer resorts. Fresh!

"We had the one grand time last year.

"I never had a more enjoyable time. Just press a button and the steward was right on the job to take your order.

"Anything from a glass of hops to a Merry Widow cocktail, and you didn't have to dig once. Everything paid for ad lib.

"Ah! those happy evenings that appeal so to every true lover of Nature and well mixed drinks. To sit and listen to the lapping of the waters—and booze.

"Us girls are talking about getting a houseboat this season if we don't have to work. Of course, the chances are that it will never come off, but up to date that is the last dressing room pipe.

"We are figuring on getting a nice place within trolley distance of Broadway and then get several of our wine agent friends to stock it for us.

"We won't need much furniture—an ice box and a corkscrew are the only real necessities.

"Do you think it would cast asparagus on my character if I should reside in a houseboat unchaperoned.

"Oh, we can get the wardrobe mistress for a chaperone, but why talk shop; and besides she gets a bun on and goes to sleep in a hamper, and we girls have to pack our own bundles, and if she got soused while chaperoning the mob it would take away the otherwise proper air of refinement and leave us open to the gibes and scoffs of those who were not so fortunate as to be invited to our houseboat.

"Say, I don't want to indulge in brag or ostentation, but the gown I am going to wear to the Friar festival they are going to pull off in May is going to have some class to it.

"Wilbur—that's my betrothed—is going to be one of the main guys, and when it comes his day to get the showing keep your eye on muh.

"I think Mr. Klaw and Mr. Erlanger are just the nicest men to give the Friars the New York Theatre for the big doings.

"You want to go. All our set will be there with their hair in a braid.

"Oh, yes; Wilbur and I are getting along just splendid. We have been engaged now for nearly two weeks and have only broken it off three times.

"I went to see 'Miss Hook of Holland' the other night and Wilbur got jealous and told me that if his show wasn't good enough for me to see without having to go to others to just come across with his ring and he would cancel the engagement.

"I, being a girl of some spirit and pride, just naturally yanked Mr. Ring off and threw it at him.

"That made him hedge and before long we were cooing over a bottle of wine like a couple of turtle doves.

"You can't take any too much off these men. Keep 'em guessing; thats my system. And then they will walk sideways, so as to not overlook any bets.

"Take that Alla McSweeney for example. She falls in love and is always on the job, like Faithful Fido. Sits around the flat and gazes at his photo all day and from quitting time on she is there with her ear to the ground waiting to hear him get out of the elevator.

"That aint little Sabrina's graft.

"Nix. Wilbur calls up and I tell him to wait a minute and let him cool his heels downstairs for a while, and then when I do send for him to come up he is more glad to see me and manages to amuse himself in hunting for a stray glove or a handkerchief.

"And then sometimes when he calls up I am out, just to let him know that he is not the only star performer.

"That stunt keeps them at heel all the time and so busy trying to keep track of you that they don't have time to look for any other dame. So that it works both ways for the dealer, and a couple of tears will always copper any wrong play you make.

"This Beatrice Fairfax dope may be all right in the simple country maiden, but it don't go in the show business worth a whoop. You've got to be on your toes in this game and play no steady system.

"My, how I run on! Here I will be late for rehearsal and will have to give the stage manager an excuse and he will fall for it until some time I have got good reason for being late, and then he will call me.

"Say, is it considered au fait for a bride-about-to-be to do a little plugging for wedding presents this early in the game? Well, so long."

Sabrina in this chapter attends a beefsteak party and becomes involved in an argument with a certain party who was formerly her roommate but whom she left quietly and by night.

CHAPTER TEN

"Don't I look like a tea store chromo?" inquired Sabrina as Estelle, her maid, opened the door. "Oh, such a time I had! Never again will I go to see that Alla McSweeney. Pipe my dial! Get onto the scratch! There are some wounds that even powder cannot hide. It all started this way. The girls down at Wilbur's show decided to give a beefsteak in honor of the prima donna getting the can. Believe me, if they had let a hanging piece fall on her she would have got but half what was coming to her. Cat! Well, I should say so, dear. She spoiled the whole effect of that 'I'd Rather Be a Lemon Than a Quince' number just because she wouldn't let the pony girls share the spot in the picture. Honest, she caused more troubles than Louis Nethersole's English actors ever imagined they had.

"I met her socially several times, and she certainly was perfectly lovely to me. But when she got back on the stage, why, she even had the stagehands stepping sideways, and you know them. And the manager couldn't call his soul his own until he had loaded her into a cab and on her way. Wilbur told me that while on the road that between watching the panners in the box offices and keeping her from throwing a fit on the stage he got gray-headed. As for her maid, I can only say, 'Help that poor creature.' One time the maid pinched her foot while buttoning her shoe and what does the prima donna do but bounce her whole makeup box on the top of the maid's defenseless nob. And the way she looks on the street compared to what she does on the stage, that makeup box must certainly have been of some size. Of course I am not roasting the poor creature, for it may be temperament instead of temper, but I am merely stating what I have heard.

"But to get back to the big eat. The prima donna got too gay and when they struck New York the home office got wise and she wouldn't stand a cut in her salary, so they just naturally decorated her with the festive bug and told her to take a whirl at vaudeville or something else real mean. Say, when the news got out that she was to leave everybody was so happy that even the chorus men went out and bought each other a beer. What do you think of that? Well, anyway the mob got together after the performance and decided to celebrate the event in fitting and proper style by getting soused, and Alla kindly donated her new flat. Yes, the Judge caught a sleeper on Wall Street and she was in strong with the cop on the beat and the people on the floor below her had moved on account of the noise. Selfish people. They didn't want to do anything all night but sleep, and Alla complained that they were wearing out the steam pipe by pounding on it.

"After the show the whole outfit cleaned all the makeup off except behind the ears and took it on the lope for Alla's domicile. Me being the guest of honor, I naturally kicked in late. Gee! everybody of any importance was there, even some of the principals, and every other show in town sent at least one representative. Say, the drum was so crowded that some of the couples had to turn the fire escape into a conservatory. They would crawl out there and bombard the neighborhood with empty bottles, until the cop on the corner would rap and then for some two or three minutes the block would be as silent as a tomb.

"Wilbur of course was there in his official capacity as press agent, to not only add tone to the gathering, but to make sure that it reached the night desk of all the papers, for if these society guys get a column and a half they ought to be willing to slip us poor chorus dolls a couple of sticks and keep it from under police news.

"I was there to see that Wilbur did not, under the influence of the charming company, make any remarks that might be misconstrued by any of the assembled gathering as a declaration of love. For them dolls are always on the job and the only time they don't catch a live one is when their hands are tied. Jealous? What! Me? Not so you can notice it, but I ain't going to have anybody have anything on me, and while I caused no scenes, I left the impression that I had Wilbur trained so that he would roll over and play dead at the word of command. While these 'keep off the grass' signs don't do much good, still they run a horrible bluff. Did Wilbur get wise to this move on my part? Not on your life! If he found out that I was, figuratively speaking, riding herd on him, he would get chesty and all swelled up until it would be my painful duty to lance him. I don't know yet whether Wilbur is a rhinestone Billie or a Whisky amber Billie with a dash of bitters Billie, but I am On the Job Betty, all right, all right.

"Well, to get back to the beefsteak. After all the guests had assembled, which was maybe some 2 a.m., they started in. It was merely the ordinary stunt of beer and beefsteak and beefsteak and beer, but the hours were enlivened by the vaudeville performances of the guests. This was before the precinct sergeant knocked on the door. One old frump that must have been tramming a mace in the Roman Hanging Gardens got a yen that was doing imitations she had Elsie Janis and Gertrude Hoffman looking like a couple of false starts. Another took the hooks out of her marsel wave and did that time-worn stunt of 'Laska.' Then one of the chorus men gave an imitation of George Cohan, as usual. But that don't explain the scratches; does it?

"To go back sometime, there was a certain skirt that I used to room with in Chicago when we were both broke, but one night she went out with a bunch of siss-boom-ah! boys and came home with a large and juicy snoot full and spent the early morning hours in leaning out of the window of the apartment and whistling through her fingers to the milkmen, as well as staging a disrobing number in the middle of the room with the curtains up to such an extent that the inhabitants of the outlying districts had to wait sometime for their morning milk.

"This, naturally grated on my refined sensibilities, so the next morning while she was yet beating the hay, I packed my little suitcase and took it on the run away from there, leaving her, you might say, on the pan. I went into the pony ballet of a La Salle Theatre show—can you see me as a pony?—and I heard that she was advancing Art with a stock burlesque in South Chicago. That evening she was among those present at the aforementioned social function. And while we kissed and embraced each other with the affection of long lost sisters, still I could detect above the odor of cocktails an underlying current of soreness. So we clinched, but I took particular pains to see that we went clean in the breakaway.

"A young gentleman from Pittsburg was one of the guests and this creature naturally put herself forward to make him have a real nice time and, while I am true to Wilbur, still I think it my duty to be kind to every one. This Chicago party got the hunch that I was trying to beat her to this Pittsburg wop and she managed to get him in a corner and I could see out of the corner of my eye that she was making a strenuous effort to reveal some of my past, and, while I have never done anything that would cast a breath of suspicion on my spotless character, still I knew that this party would not hesitate for a minute to do some romancing, so I naturally edged over toward that particular corner as if I was not noticing myself do it, and overheard her inform the gent, that while I had the outward appearance of an innocent young babe, I was a viper at heart, and had beat it out of Chicago with some ten or twelve thousand dollars' worth of her personal jewelry.

"Shucks! All the jewelry she ever had was a diamond stickpin she bit out of a gentleman's scarf when they were going home in a cab, and all she had left of that was the pawn ticket.

"Naturally hearing the libelous remarks, I was compelled to defend myself, so I quietly interrupted her conversation by remarking lightly over her shoulder, 'Ah! I see, Laura, that you are still a member of the Arm and Hammer band, and I wish to mention in passing that the only ten or twelve thousand dollars' worth of jewelry you ever had you returned to the property man every night after the ballroom scene.'

"As for me eloping with your belongings all you ever had was a dirty handkerchief kimona, a Fluffy Ruffles skirt and a near-seal jacket, and you had to throw a chill when you entered a cafe so as not to have to take that off. If you had you would have been disgraced for life."

After those kind remarks Laura's goat naturally make a quick exit. She jumped to her feet, and with one of those 'Parted on Her Bridal Tour' expressions, said: 'It's you, is it, Sabrina; you were always noted as the Butting-in Kid. But now if you have got all of that humorous monologue of yours out of your system you can toddle right along and sell your matches, as this kind gentleman and I are discussing a few words in private and do not wish them to get all over town.'

"'Can that chatter,' said I, 'and don't forget the happy days you spent at Sid Euson's.' Right there is where I got that scratch. But I being pretty nifty with my fins gave her a cuff on the chops that she won't have to put down in her diary to remember. I was just fishing for an opening to land when Wilbur stayed my upraised arm, and I could only give her a kick on the limb with my French heel. Naturally the noise and the words attracted some attention even from that bunch; that is, it could be heard above the usual hum of conversation. The dame, knowing that I was in the right, tried to tuck the Pittsburg party under her arm and duck the dump, but Pittsburg being a game guy, stuck for the big show, and Laura loped for the 'L' alone.

"Wilbur was naturally surprised and grieved at my actions, and for a moment allowed the green-eyed monster to take up standing room in his heart, thinking that I had succumbed to the wealth of the coal dealer, but my ready outburst of maidenly tears quickly set me to rights. That was the only thing that marred the evening, except one of the girls spoke kindly to a chorus man, and he, poor fellow, threw a fainting fit and we had to force the only jig juice in the crowd between his clinched teeth before he could be revived.

"Yes, I am still on the stage, but I have got the stage manager trained so that I only have to slip him a five spot any night I fail to appear. No, there isn't much doing except that some of the girls are rehearsing for the soul kiss contest, but I personally do not have to advertise.

"What! Going? Say, on your way down tell the barhop to mix me up a life preserver in a rose glass."

Sabrina touches on the advantages of having a hotel for chorus girls and makes several comments on the dramatic possibilities of "The Mangled Doughnut," with which she is rehearsing.

CHAPTER ELEVEN

"Say," remarked Sabrina, as we met her in front of her favorite cafe, "say, loosen up, cough, give down, come to, kick in. You've got to donate for a couple of tickets to the annual benefit of the Unemployed or Otherwise Disabled Chorus Girls' Home, and the quicker you come across the quicker your suffering will be over. Sure we are going to have a benefit that will make even the Friar Festival get up and hump itself. And you know that's going to be some show. The Chorus Girls' Mutual Knocking Society is going to build a home so that the poor doll who comes in from the high grass in her normal condition, broke, can have some place to go and rest and refresh herself without having to hock a couple of wedding rings before she can have her hotel trunk sent up.

"There's going to be fifty sleeping rooms and ninety-six maids, so that if the poor skirt wakes up in the morning feeling far from a well woman all she has to do is to tickle the zing-zing and the maid is right there on the job. There is to be nineteen sound-proof parlors with two pianos in each parlor.

"While there will be a chaperon, of course, she will permit the young ladies to entertain their friends in a quiet and ladylike manner until the porter starts cleaning up the bar in the morning. The inmates will of course be allowed to sign checks, but from visitors only cash will be accepted.

"Can you see a mob of those merry dames around that drum? Talk about your something doing every minute! Say, it will look like open time around that shack. Burlesquers are canceled. They can't come into the home. Well, they never have much of a home anyway, so they don't miss much.

"Burlesque is sure one strenuous existence. Mother made me quit. That and the doctor telling me that I would ruin myself standing around a draughty stage in tights. And besides those burlesque stage hands certainly are cruel. Why, you have to put the money right in their hand before they will beat it across the alley for a can of suds. If that ain't cruelty I don't know what is. Do they think us girls would enjoy our refreshment if we have to pay for it ourselves. Why, it hasn't got the same flavor. Do you think a girl lacks class when she puts salt in her beer?

"That home will be a great thing. Imagine going home every night without wondering if your room is locked and the landlady sitting on your trunks at the top landing. You can just flounce into your nest any old time and know that everything is right there, unless one crafty girl has bribed the chambermaid for the key. You can never tell about those people. Why, I know one girl who kept stealing hairs out of the different wigs in the dressing-rooms until she had enough to make a Dutch braid, and then she put on such a front and chest that she wouldn't speak to any of the other girls should she happen to meet them socially. I have always wanted a home, not that I haven't been offered several, but I mean a permanent one. But to continue about the benefit.

"Wilbur is going to manage it, and he expects to shake down enough to start us housekeeping, but, of course, that is strictly under your hat, and I pray you do not mention it. I think we can get Mr. Erlanger to let us use the New York Theatre if we promise not to damage the fixtures. He lets every other benefit have it and he certainly wouldn't object to a few poor chorus girls pulling off a shindy, seeing as how they did so much for his success.

"Suppose none of us had gone on in the chorus of 'Ben-Hur'? Just think what would have happened. Didn't know there was a chorus in 'Ben-Hur'? Say, what are you trying to do, kid me, or just show me a good time?

"I was around yesterday trying to get some of the oldtime merry-merry who are now some of our leading actresses to appear at the benefit, but they all threw a fit at the mere mention of the fact that they had once carried a spear. For my part I see nothing degrading in the work, even if we are held up to the gibes and chaff of some of these newspaper near-humorists.

"It certainly is an honorable calling, and if you look good from the front you can always have your pick of the menu. So that any dame that can hand out the frightened fawn glance need never starve.

"Ain't it funny the way these Johns stick their noses to the ground and start on the trail of 'the soldiers, villagers, etc.'? They'll pass up anything just to be able to stick their arm through the stage door and hand the doorkeeper a bunch of violets.

"They will leave Flossie, the belle of the village, waiting at the gate any time a burlesque three-sheet shows up on the side of the blacksmith shop. And right down front, with their feet on the base drum, handing out the coy glances before the first curtain is a foot from the stage.

"Yep, I'm still rehearsing with 'The Mangled Doughnut,' and the author of the book told me yesterday, in the strictest confidence, that it will be the best first-night performance Hartford ever saw.

"He says he expects to stay up all that night rewriting the book, but he is willing to sacrifice a few hours' sleep in the interest of Art. And for the musical numbers, as we are rehearsing forty-two songs, some of them ought to go. The only thing wrong with the show as far as I can see is that the prima donna acts like she was in a trance. It is my personal opinion—of course I wouldn't have you breathe this to a living soul for worlds—but it is my personal opinion that she sniffs the white. She either does that or jabs, though it don't show on her arm. The leading comedian is a sad affair.

"He would make a good understudy for a morgue, and that's about all. Why, I offered him suggestions for some new business in his cafe scene and he went up-stage on the run and informed me that when he desired instructions from the chorus concerning the way to handle his part he would address me in writing. I said to him: 'Far be it from me to get gay, old top, but I would respectfully suggest that you get busy with the pen and ink.' Then he was going to have me fired. Such a chance.

"He had better find out what I know about the past history of the person who hired me before he hands out any lurid language about my dismissal. I know right where I stand, and though I am one of the shop girls in the first act, instead of having my regular place as an American heiress, I know right where I stand every shake out of the box.

"Viola St. Clare is sure having the one strenuous time with her new husband. The poor dear is nearly balmy in the crumpet from worry. You see, they have been married but four long weeks, and the last three nights he has been coming home sober, and she believes he is deceiving her, so she is trying to get enough money from him so that she can hire a private detective to have him shadowed.

"They tell me that Sam Harris has to punch a time clock. I know one thing, and that is when I am married Wilbur will not be one of the leading lights of the Knickerbocker, even if I have to prance down there and drag him out by the neck. Gee, there ain't much doing in town now. Wilbur and a couple of friends are already running trial heats for the Twenty-three Club dinner, and if he ever recovers from that our engagement will be announced. I am having the photographs taken now.

"Tell me, do you think it's good form for a lady to have her wedding announcement accompanied by pictures of herself in tights. Wilbur says that it won't help me, but it will do the show a lot of good, and he says somebody connected with my show should be done good besides the manager.

"I will say one good word about our show—it has a grand first act. The other two acts may be on the cheese, but the first act is good. The author says the first act of a show is the only one that needs any attention, because it is the only one the critics ever stick for anyway. We got great scenery; the second act is made of what you might call a composite set, being composed out of all the scenery from the other failures this year.

"Did I say other failures?"

"I spoke inadvertently. 'For this elaborate production, with its all-star cast of metropolitan favorites and its famous beauty chorus,' as Wilbur says, may be all right.

"Mind you, I only say may.

"The first act is laid in a quince plantation, and the quinces of the chorus are discovered at curtain rise picking the luscious fruit. There is a naval vessel in the harbor. This was put in so the tenor could wear his white duck uniform; he had to wear something, and when the management found that he had a white duck uniform—every tenor has, you know, or he wouldn't be a tenor—when the management found that he had a uniform they took the money they had advanced for costumes away from him and rewrote the first act.

"As I say, we lemons are picking quinces or we quinces are picking lemons, any way you want to take it, and after finishing the opening chorus we rush up stage, open center, and in comes the prima donna in a pony cart—a stone boat would suit her better, but that is neither here nor there—see pony cart, chance for number by pony ballet, with six trained doughnuts—you see that's where the title of the play is introduced. That's the only time the title shows up except a duet between the leading lady and the tenor entitled 'I Had Rather be a Doughnut in Harlem Than a Butter Cake in Childs'.'

"The prima and the tenor do an imitation of the 'Merry Widow' waltz. The author didn't want that put in, but the backer of the show convinced him that nowadays every true musical comedy had an imitation of the 'Merry Widow' waltz, so he let it slide.

"After that in comes the comedian as the valet of a wealthy American just arrived on the battleship.

"He has got a great entrance. It's brought out by some plot lines spoken by two of the chorus girls that he has taken a taxaballoon from the boat and while up in the air he bites the rope of the balloon in two in a fit and falls center stage with a red spotlight on him. That's the musical cue for his song.

"'I'd Rather Be Up in the Air Than Up in the Bronx.' He has learned twenty-two extra verses and says that he will give them all if the ushers' hands hold out.

"When he is through in comes the soubrette, formerly a lady boilermaker in Canarsie, but now disguised as an adventuress, in search of the missing papers.

"She has the papers in a locket given her by her mother, but don't know it until the comedian bites her on the neck in the third act and breaks the chain, when the locket falls to the ground and the papers fall out.

"The second act is a scene in Maxim's, where the leading lady is washing dishes. That gives more comedy, with the comedian as a dish.

"The American is hiding from his wife and goes to Maxim's because he knows she'll be there. If she wasn't, shucks! There wouldn't be no show.

"He does his specialty with a piece of cheese—not the prima donna—and after that the American Beauty Chorus comes in and does a refined can-can.

"My how I have run on! I just know I'll be late for rehearsal, but don't forget the benefit. We need the money, Wilbur and me. So long!"

In which Sabrina prepares to leave town with the show, but pauses to pass a few remarks on love, comedians, murders, maids, spring millinery and the advisability of anyone marrying their first husband.

CHAPTER TWELVE

"Goodbye, dear," said Sabrina, as we met her hurrying up Broadway. "Our show leaves town to-morrow. We got to get to Hartford in time for a dress rehearsal before the evening performance. My, such a time we have had. You know the comedian we had threw up the sponge at the last minute and we had to dig up another. Thank goodness, this one is a gentleman and not getting fresh with the merry-merry every time he gets a chance.

"Oh, say, was you at the Friars' Sunday Night in Bohemia a couple of weeks ago? The Friars spend every night in Bohemia or the Knickerbocker bar, so Wilbur says. But honest, this was a great stunt, seconded only by the Festival they are going to pull off in May.

"The curtain went up on what looked like a busy day in Childs', and Wells Hawks was in the spotlight, surrounded by a bevy of blondes and empty champagne bottles. They tell me that Gus Edwards had to blindfold Hawks to lead him up to the table where the empty bottles were, and as for the girls, it was with a great effort that they restrained themselves.

"All they could do was to look at the empty bottles, hold their noses and drink mineral water. Ain't it awful, Mabel? Anyway, everybody had a good time, so what care they for gibes and jeers? Many the time have I held a champagne cork to my nose, closed my eyes and dreamed that I was having a time. Well, to continue about our show. Wilbur says it will never go, because they only got block stands, and an agent ain't got no show without at least one kind of a litho. Wilbur said it hurt the artistic instinct of a billposter in these hick towns to put up all block stands, and you generally have to slip them a little something to be sure that they burn up all the extra stuff, so that the manager of the company wouldn't find it should he go snooping around the bill room when the show gets in town. He says if they get a good litho of a killing or a chorus they will go out of the way to stick them up just for art's sake. Wilbur is going to give me a suit case full of hard tickets to the Friar Festival, and told me to mace every John I came across on the road for as many as he would stand for. He said the more I sent in the more he would know I loved him. Wilbur is so romantic!

"This new comedian we got with the show is pretty good, but of course I can see defects. And the new prima donna is real nice. She asked me into her dressing-room the other afternoon and slipped me a little idea encourager that she had in a flask. But the way she is in love with the tenor, honest, it's sickening to me. She watches him from the time he comes in the theatre until the time he leaves, and then calls him up on the 'phone at his home.

"The other day when he asked one of the girls to tie the ribbon in his cuff she got so jealous that I thought she was going to give the poor kid a lam on the lamp. What she can see in that tenor is beyond me. What anybody can see in a tenor has got me guessing, for that matter. Wilbur says that's just the way with temperamental people, and he lost a job once just because he forgot to land pictures in the Sunday editions of all the newspapers in town of the manager's own particular guiding star, but planted a bunch of her dearest friend instead. He says there's no pleasing them, and the only way to have peace and harmony around the whole show shop is to print flashlights of the entire company. And even that looks like blazes, for the editor will always reduce an eight-column flashlight to a two-column cut, no matter how many drinks you buy him.

"He says he saw a murder once—was the only witness, in fact—and he took it on the run to a newspaper office and offered to trade a Charles Sommerville to the editor for a reading notice about the show, and the editor told him that they could get all they wanted from the police, and what they didn't get wouldn't hurt the public if they didn't know about it. He says if that wouldn't give the press agent art a kick in the neck nothing would.

"Wilbur says he loves his art and nothing pleases him better than to find a box office that will take his I O U. Us chorus have been sure working hard the past week, and Ben Teal has been just that kind and gentle, and didn't put a one of us on the pan. We certainly have got some lovely costumes; they ain't much to them, but what there is is beautiful. They smell a little of camphor, but they have been packed away in hampers ever since last season, and that accounts for it.

"I got a fine scene with the comedian and should score a great personal triumph. All of us girls are lined up for his entrance in the second act, and when he comes in he walks right over to me and says: 'Ah, little one. How are you on the Queen's wedding day,' 'Queen's wedding day,' that's my cue, and

I say, 'Very well, thank you kindly, noble sire.' Aint that great? It takes nearly a whole side. I was rehearsing it in my apartment this morning with Estelle, but she was so rotten as the comedian that I took away the last $5 I gave her for a tip.

"These menials have no talent in their souls. Estelle, that's my maid, says she has no desire to elevate the drama, and she had rather be a maid for a chorus girl any time—there's more money in it. She may be right at that.

"Alla McSweeney is going to start a New Thought Church. She says that she has a whole flock of new thoughts and it would be quite fashionable to start this new think stunt. She said she would tell us her new thoughts if she thought we would never breathe a word to a living breathing soul. Gee, that lets our gang out.

"They couldn't keep quiet if it killed them. Honest, for a bunch of knockers, perfect both in single handed knocking and team work, our set has anything bound to the bannister in New York.

"But what care I? Spring is coming and we will all soon hike to Bath Beach. Honest, for a country place with all the conveniences of home Bath Beach is the top liner. You can put a can under your shawl and rush a couple of blocks and always get it full of the best, and if you put butter around the side of the pail the barkeep ignores the fact and goes right ahead.

"I may get a motor boat this summer if Wilbur gets his summer snap at the island.

"Coney, I mean, not Blackwell's.

"He has never been over there except to take flowers to the Poillon sisters. They love nature so. Charlotte says it makes her homesick every time she sees a Joy Line boat go by.

"The benefit season will soon open and any person that has a couple of thousand dollars to pay for a theater can git a benefit for himself and maybe draw down a couple of hundred more. The benefit for the chorus, girls has gone up in the air, for none of them would acknowledge that they were chorus girls.

"They were either show girls or pony dancers, and that let them out. Anyway, each girl wanted to bring her maid, and the dressing rooms would have been so full of maids that there would have been no room for the dolls. I had it all framed up, too. I had six wine agents and a whisky salesman who guaranteed to appear, and that alone would have made the thing a financial success. But what could I do?

"Our bunch has been rehearsing five weeks without salaries, and with the excessive taxicab rates we got no money to spend on clothes to wear to the ball, and the wardrobe mistress keeps an awful tab on the costume hampers.

"A certain friend of mine, who, by the way, I wouldn't trust any further than I can throw an elephant by the tail, had the nerve to take me up in her apartment the other day and show me her new bathing suit she had just imported from Paris. It was a swell thing all right, but sewed in the waistband was a piece of cloth that said 'Burgomaster 2' on it, so you can draw your own conclusions.

"Honest, the way some girls steal is something awful. Take it from me, it's nothing less than stealing to swipe a wardrobe. Of course, if the show is going to close it's all right, but from a successful production, never. Lifting a scarfpin from a soused party is all right, for he is supposed to do something to remunerate the lady for wasting her time by taking her to supper.

"Spring has sure come and I do just glory in nature. I suppose that is because I was brought up in the country. We never have anything but nature in Emporia.

"Oh, I heard from the folks the other day, and they tell me that Emporia is now growing to be some town. The bank is putting up a four-story brick building, which is going to be looked on as the village skyscraper.

"The town council has already passed resolutions restricting the height of the buildings to six stories. They ain't going to take the chance that New York does, and have some of these big tall ten-story affairs topple over into their streets.

"All the yaps out in that neighborhood are lining out for the spring plowing now while the yaps here are lining out for the spring millinery openings. I already got the dressmaker on the job for seven or eight modest little frocks that will make them sit up and take notice Sundays down at Manhattan Beach.

"I have decided that I am going to be an athletic girl this summer, and am already taking exercise every day. Why, I walk all the way from the subway to the hotel, and that's nearly half a block.

"Say, what do you know about this? Posey Golden has married her first husband.

"Honest! You know they were divorced shortly after she got a good job, and have been living apart ever since.

"She married again to the nicest gambler you ever met. But he got stung on a sleeper, and had to hock the family jewels, and Posey said that was cruelty, for she could never have the face to go down to the dining room for breakfast without all of her diamonds on; she had worn them every day since they struck the St. Reckless, and she was afraid it might cause talk among the waiters and guests because she always treated them with a calm air of condescension, and they would lay for the chance to get in a hammer. So she put in a bid for a divorce and got it.

"Then she met her first better half on the street and, after having a little supper, they decided to sneak through the tunnel, take it on the run for Newark and again become one.

"Imagine anybody going to Newark to get married! Imagine any one going to Newark for anything!

"They got married and came back to town just as happy as if nothing had ever happened. My, I hope Wilbur and I will be that way! I think he is sincere even if he does write good notices about girls in his show.

"Well, I must toddle along and see if Wilbur has cashed his yet, so that I can get the rest of that new hat. If it ain't too much trouble you can send me a bunch of flowers for our opening night in Hartford. So long."

The show gives its opening performance and Sabrina scores a great personal success. She speaks at some length of the kissing craze and makes several comments on the time she had while out of town.

CHAPTER THIRTEEN

"Are you coming to the opening tonight?" began Sabrina, the Show Girl, before she had given her order. "I don't know if you can get a seat or not, because the management is tired of having the same old gang out in front, and have donated about two-thirds of the house to the ladies at the Martha Washington, for they know more about a real show than anybody, because they read the dramatic page of all the fashion magazines, and the other third of the house will be taken up by the dramatic critics and their friends.

"We had a great opening in Hartford. The theatre was crowded four rows back. The first act went great, but we couldn't tell how the last one went, because nobody but the author and composer stayed for it, and they are a little partial.

"I scored a great personal triumph, and the way I read my lines was not only greeted with applause, but with laughter. In fact, I made such a decided hit that the prima donna, who, by the way, is worse than the first, because she drinks, had the manager take my lines away from me and give them to somebody who could not read them as well. If I wasn't afraid she would blackball me for the P.W.L. I would raise a kick. The idea of an old frump like that letting professional jealousy interfere with Art.

"After the performance that night the author got busy and rewrote the whole second act, and had it all ready by the time we landed in Washington.

"Do you think we get a chance to rush around and mingle with the Congressmen and other such truck? Not on your life. It was to the show shop for us and do the big rehearsal all day, and we only had time to slip out and soak up a sandwich and get back in time for the evening's performance.

"I changed my tights from blue to pink for the first night and scored another personal triumph. So much so that the soubrette made it a point to stand in front of me every time she did a number with the chorus. She belonged over on the other side in front of the Glonesganes creature, in order to dress the stage, and the manager jumped all over her for moving.

"The show went big that night, and the next day some of the critics spoke favorably of it. I don't care what they say, it's a good show, and as the plot has been almost entirely eliminated it should go well here.

"After rehearsing all day Tuesday we were allowed to walk up and down Pennsylvania avenue and get acquainted. I met a gentleman who said he had been introduced to me in New York, and he certainly treated me grand. We went over to the Willard for supper, and he just tossed the menu toward me, careless like, and said, 'Got to it, kid.' Talk about your Southern gallantry! A bunch of these near-sports will rush a girl into a feedshop, and they have no more than got seated at the table before he will commence talking about the big dinner he has just had, so that the poor thing feels like a burglar if she eats anything more than a couple of lobsters. But not this Percival, he frankly admitted that he hadn't had anything to eat for a week and scratched no entries.

"I wish these New Yorkers were that way—nothing personal dear—but they have become so callous to feeding the merry-merry that they have the big eat dodging stunt down to a science. The only way to get more than a two-dollar, including wine, feed out of most of these moss-covered pocketbooks is by blasting.

"Why, I have known certain parties to adopt the subterfuge of going out to telephone and then beating it to avoid paying the check. Thus leaving the poor feedee to pay the bill or wait longingly for a friend to show up on the horizon.

"A gentleman who will pull off a deal like that is not worthy of the confidence of one of our sex. But, understand, I am not by any means damning the whole male sex, for I have met gentlemen who threw the lid of their grouch bag in the gutter and didn't care if they ever found it again. Those is the kind of parties that has my trust. Me grub, and I got money in the bank? Sure I do. I got to keep in training somehow, so if I did lose my inheritance I wouldn't be out of practice.

"Wilbur don't blame me for it. He says that the object in life of an agent and a chorus girl is to plant everything they can get their fins into whenever they can, for it don't last long, and the good people ain't healthy. And goodness knows I sure do need my health. For though I appear to be a strong, robust creature I am a frail woman.

"Wilbur can moan and groan around with a hangover for a couple of days, but I have to be right on the job all the time with this smiling face and laughing eye thing, or he would seek some other place for sympathy. Why, many a morning I have spoke light and happy words of cheer to him over the 'phone with a tongue as thick as a board-walk and the inside of my nob yearning to burst loose and flop around in the cool morning air.

"Do I caper up to the transmitter and sob, 'Oh, darling, I fear me that I am not long for this earth!' Never! I take a long drink of ice water, and when his 'Is this you, kid?' comes over the wire I chirrup back, real bright and gay, 'Right O, Kiddo!' and when he says he don't believe he can live through the day, do I suggest that we die together? Not I! I tell him to forget it and go downstairs and have George mix him up a mug full of the hair of the dog that bit him. That shows the love of a good woman.

"Was you at the Chorus Girls' Ball last Saturday night? My, I would hate to cast any reflections on the judges, but their choice certainly was bum. Still I suppose they are old men and not up on the modern 1908 rules on osculation.

"In their day when a young man imprinted a chaste salute on a dame's alabaster forehead he was supposed to go into a fit of delight, but not according to this year's book. Now they clinch with a strangle hold and stick till one or the other drops from exhaustion. I did not enter the contest, for I am not a chorus girl; I am a show girl, if you please. What's the difference? Five a week.

"This kissing craze is getting to be something scandalous. Not that I object to it. But I blush to think that the time-honored customs that were once performed in the front parlor, with the gas turned low, is now used in contests and numbered as a feat of strength.

"Wilbur and I went to the ball together, and as soon as he struck the hut he wanted to rush right over and run a few trial heats with the contestants, but the easy way with which I made him change his mind was a joy to the eye. He said to me as we went in the door, I think I will toddle over to the paddock and see if the fillies are in form. He was making a wild rush to check his shawl when I mentioned casual like, as if I wasn't noticing myself saying it, 'You know that I am an added starter.' Bing! Skyrockets! Wilbur goes up in the air and comes down all spraddled out.

"'What!' he pipes, as soon as he got his breath, 'my financed bride billed to appear in a hugging handicap? Not yet! Sabrina you certainly do jag my jib to think that you would enter into such a deal. From now on our trail parts.' 'Oh, I don't know,' I said. 'What's sauce for the goose is sauce for the gander, and if you pull off any stunts you can figure that I will be in the running. And that goes as it lays.'

"That was no nice language for a lady, but it put the brakes on Wilbur's osculatory aspirations so quick that he stopped with a jolt. He canceled the date and we went up into the box and stood in the receiving line for wine agents.

"Wilbur knew that he had to stand hitched or I wouldn't let him go to the Twenty-three Club dinner tonight. He has been training for the event for the last two weeks, and he says that he will be able to outdistance the bunch before 4 a.m., and you know that's going some.

"It's a pity they wouldn't let us women in on their feed deals. They go out and fill up on beefsteak while we have to stick around and drown our sorrows in a cheese sandwich. And goodness knows that while they are nourishing they don't give you any new ideas.

"I only hope our show is a success, for if Wilbur and I get married every penny will help, and I don't want to lance my personal fresh air fund for anything more than a bridal veil. Wilbur and I are just like two doves, but I am taking no chances, for press agents are fickle people.

"With all due regard to Wilbur's feelings I must say that the agent of our company is a dog. He had the nerve to come up to us girls and want us to beat it up and down Broadway with signs boosting the show on our backs. A doll would stand a swell chance in Jack's with a big sign reading, 'Go see 'The Abused Cruller' at the Folly' on her vertebrae, now wouldn't she?

"Can you see me as the walking three-sheet? I make exhibition enough of myself on the stage without prancing up and down with one of those things tied to my Fluffy Ruffles.

"I just had an awful time in Washington. One of the girls that dresses in the same room with me came in with one of those crying buns on and shed so many weeps in my makeup box that I had to put it on with an atomizer.

"I did all a human being could do to bring her to—rubbed her hands and slapped her face; but even then she was in no fit condition to appear. Go on she would, in spite of my prayers, and what does she do when she comes tripping on, blithe and gay as a school girl, but stumble and do a slide on her profile half way across the O.P. side, just as the tenor was starting the chorus to his song, 'Bevey in Little Children.' He being a nervous party springs a blue note that got the musical director hysterical and he forgot to give the bass drum man his cue and the whole thing went to blazes.

"It was lucky that the stage manager was making a date on the dressing room stairs, or what she would have got would have been a-plenty.

"You know Laura O'Toole who was married a few weeks ago? Well, she is again a widow. Her husband got a job with a road show. She was thinking of wearing mourning, but her husband staked her to the price of a new spring suit and she said that conventionalities could go hang, as she had a shape and was going to show it. I don't blame her. Why let grief put it on style?

"Gee, it won't be long before summer, and then we will get our salaries reduced. That's the trouble with the people I work for. Every time they get a success here in town they start to reduce salaries. If the company would stand for it we would be owing them money every week before the end of the season. They think a girl hasn't nothing to do but ride around in an automobile and look sweet.

"Well, me to get on the war paint. Say, have you offered your services for the Friar Festival yet? Well, you had better get on the job if you want to consider yourself classy. So long! Oh, you know the ushers will hand flowers over the footlights if you just tell him who they are for. Bye-bye."

The show opens on Broadway and Sabrina shows surprise at the number of harsh words in the English language. She discloses the methods of the Lease Breakers Association and mentions the events that transpired at a little informal gathering.

CHAPTER FOURTEEN

"My, did you see what the critics said about our show?" exclaimed Sabrina, Show Girl, as her maid opened the door. "Wasn't it awful? I didn't know there were so many mean words in the book. And the nerve of them to pan me after meeting several of them socially. One of them said that I looked so good standing up that it was a crime to have me sit down, but when I spoke for goodness sake get the muffler. The mut! I should go down and horsewhip him. But no, that's what us people that figure in public are bound to get. They never say a good word until after the minister says, 'Dust thou art to dust returneth,' and then some cluck is liable to come along and dig up a bunch of letters.

"I am thinking seriously of taking a flat until summer. I don't like this hotel, one has to keep so many conventionalities. Why, the other day my 'phone was out of order and I ran down to the desk in my kimona to telephone and the clerk had the nerve to call me for it. Can you surpass that? I told him to open his ears and let his head cool off.

"I was looking at a nice flat the other day, but they want me to sign a lease. What do I know about a lease? There ain't no half salary clause in it. If I did sign the lease and want to beat it all I would do would be to call in the Lease Breakers' Association and I could leave the next day. That mob responds to a call like the crowd in the Cadillac when some one says, I'll buy,' and you can take it from me that's going some.

"Sure, haven't you heard of the Lease Breakers' Association? They guarantee to break any lease in less than a week. It is composed of a mob of select ladies and gentlemen who can make the most noise. A person wishing to leave their abode and handicapped with a lease has but to blow the whistle for this gang and furnish plenty of refreshments and there is nothing to it. I attended one the other evening and we all had the one grand time.

"A friend of mine has ceased being married and naturally has no more use for a whole flat, so she approached the cruel landlord and asked for a release.

Did she get it? Not. He told her that she would have to stick or stand the consequences. Does she tear out a bunch of hair and rave all over the room? Not her. She gets the members of the Lease Breakers on the 'phone and that night they hold the big celebration and the next morning four tenants kicked to the landlord. The morning after that the whole building kicked in a body and the janitor had to repair two ceilings. Then the guv asked her to move and she refused until he gave up her month's rent. She was foolish like one of those birds they call a fox. I guess, yes. These landlords have to go some if they want to get ahead of the simple Bohemians. What they want rent for beats me. They own the houses and that ought to satisfy them.

"If I do get this flat, take it from me, we will pull off the grand one time. I intend to hold a reception every evening after the show until I get a request to move.

"Say, here's the big jest in our set. You know, Olga Jones and her husband don't get along very well together. Their temperaments don't jibe.

"Well, her soul mate and she had given hubby the slip and were down in my apartments putting on the finishing touches to the big eats. Soul Mate was telling the story of his life to Olga when in kicks the dame that Soul Mate had formerly been in love with.

"They are both wise people and neither tip their mit, though Soul Mate grew restless with his feet. This was about 4 a.m. and the mere shank of the evening, as it were. When all of a sudden, Bing! Bing! on the door and in waltzed Olga's handicap, who had been out and soaked up a souse, and not finding little wifey when he returned to the hut, he starts out on a still hunt and ropes in my shack.

"Hubby comes in carrying weight for grouch and pipes party of five— Blonde Party, Olga, Soul Mate, Wilbur and me. Calls down wifey for not coming home. Business of language. I kick in and tells him to have a drink. Nothing to it. Oil on the troubled waters looked like an also ran.

"Hubby was perfectly content and after a drink or two he beat it, telling wifey to hurry home. Fine. Blonde Party finds she is fifth wheel and also ducks. Then Olga lands on Soul Mate. 'Who is this peroxide party?'

"'Only an old passing fancy,' chirrups Soul Mate.

"Olga tears her hair and bites out a bunch of hectic language about having the only man she ever loved being false, and how life is naught but a hollow bubble and all that kind of rot. Wilbur having sporting blood was for kidding them on and seeing if they would mix it, but me desiring peace and quiet told what I didn't know about the affair and squared things. Business of embracing.

"Did you pipe the sassy half-sheets Mr. McManus got out for the Friar Festival? Ain't they just too pretty for words? Do you know who that guy reading the Friar song down in the corner is? Don't breathe a word and I'll tell you. It's Phil Mindel. Honest it is. George sketched it from life one night over at the Booze Arts.

"Us chorus girls were talking of marching to Albany in a body with drums beating and flags flying and demanding that the anti-betting bill be ditched. It is something fierce the way these reformers are trying to put the bee on our pleasures.

"I just dote on horse races. Why, I can go to the track and sit in the cafe for hours. I wonder what these guys think we are going to do with our spare time this summer? Sit at home and make sofa pillows? Why, there is no greater sport in the world than riding out to Sheepshead or Jamaica in an auto and then borrowing money from your escort to bet on the patty-pats. It's a great system. If you lose the John gets nothing, and if you win you take everything, so it is fair for all parties.

"If they want to do something truly noble they should put those moving picture shows out of business. Pretty soon when they want the chorus to show up they will let down a sheet, throw on the picture and turn loose, 'Welcome, your highness, welcome' on the phonograph. I ain't mentioning any names, but there is a bunch of these parties that belong on a moving picture.

"What do you know about the circus? Ain't it all to the pickles? Me there the other matinee in a real box, courtesy of the management. Did you get your attention called to the two Janes that did the ride in the hurdics down the hill? Some class to that act. Imagine looping the loop in the air! Not for Sabrina, the pride of the chorus. As long as I can make my living on my shape you don't catch me trying to damage it soaring around in the atmosphere. Not for five dollars more a week, as bad as I need the money.

"I went to see Wells Hawks and the elephants. Both of them are permanent fixtures, though they do say that he is kept busy looking after the animals at both the Hip. and the circus. And the clowns! May I be struck dead if I didn't just rear back and howl my head off at those crazy clucks.

"Alla McSweeney certainly is a sneeze. She has no idea of the fitness of things. I was telling her just the other day. I said, 'Alla, you certainly are no piker. You'll go out and mace a good fellow for a big feed just as if he was a John. Now, that ain't right. When you are out with a James go to it and eat your head off. But when you are out with some one in the business or a newspaper man be circumscribe. Though you may want to wade through the whole dope sheet hitch your desire and order what you think he can afford, and lay back until you get a live one.'

"What? Sure we do. If a Jane goes out with a John that has nothing but. Nothing's too good for her and walking is hard on the feet. The more money the wop spends the bigger sport he thinks he is, but a fellow professional has honorable intentions, sometimes, and it is considered wise not to show what you are accustomed to until after he has bought the ring or written some letters. I may go out with some fellow and order everything from soup to nuts just to show him that I can, but the way I won Wilbur's heart was by ordering a cheese sandwich the first time he invited me out.

"My goodness! How I run on, and here it is getting late. Well, I must toddle along and see how the Friar Festival is. I have a personal interest in that. So long. Say, the next time you expect to get lanced for the big feed tell her you were once in the business and it will save you money. Ta, ta."

In which Sabrina has a row with the stage-manager, leaves the show, frivols in the vineyard, denounces the male sex as being all alike, threatens, to take the veil, but finally falls upon the neck of her betrothed and all is forgotten.

CHAPTER FIFTEEN

We came upon Sabrina seated alone at a table in the rear of a cafe; her hat was tilted rakishly over one ear, a couple of strands of hair were hanging down over her forehead, a bright spot glowed on each cheek and her eyes had a dim, moist appearance. The table was covered with glasses and bottles and the chairs looked as if they had been hastily shoved back.

As we approached her she waved her hand joyfully and exclaimed, 'Welcome bri' Springtime. Wel-come to our country village. You—you behold in me the only living survivor of the wreck of the Hesperus. Parade ri' up, and give the waiter your hat, coat and vest and bevy in. Though I have just given nineteen dollars' worth of hair puffs away as sou-sou-ven—you say it, I feel like a new born child. Once again I am care fre' and heart fre'. Tra la la la le. I have just decorated Wilbur with the sacred order of the bee and I—hurray! hurray!—am no longer a near-bride. Take it fr'm muh I feel so happy I don' care if I get spots all over the fron' of my waist. I feel like a lark. Yes shur, a bottled-in-bond lark. Whatever that ish. An' I still got the engagemen' ring at that.

"Waiter! Waiter! Garsong! Thish gentleman has a few words to shay to you, an' don' take no for an answer. Oh, yes, you arch your eyebrows in sus-sus-picioning and shay that I have been two-stepping around the juniper bowl and I will answer, 'Right O!' Just like that.

"I make it a rule to cel'brate all suspicious occasions by revelry and goo' cheer. Oh, won' I have a head in the morning! But now.

"Behold I appear as Columbine! I toil not neither do I spin. Listen, my dear. The last two days have been fraught—whatever that is—with incidences that would bring gray hairs to the head of much stronger women than I.

"It came off last night. I was out to supper with a couple of gentlemen— Wilbur and an-another gent. We were so busy talking things over that I didn't get to the theater until the middle of the first act. My, I never saw a man so peevish as that stage manager. I had no more than exchanged the courtesies of the day with the stage doorkeeper and asked after his sick child than that mut-faced sneeze that calls himself a stage manager had the nerve to rush up an fine me five dollars. Wha'da you think of that?

"I told him that I positively refused to appear the rest of the evening. Then he told me that I was fired? What do you know about that? I said, calm and dignified, like the perfec' lady I am, 'All ri', you can do as you please with your old show, I don't care, I don't care, nothing bothers me,' and with those kind words I caper up to the dressing room and take that expensive gown I wear in the third act and stuck it in the wash bowl and turned on the water. It needed cleaning anyway. Then I put a few things that oughta belong to me in my makeup box and beat it.

"I had to kiss everybody in the company goo' bye and that made the stage wait and the manager came chasing around without any goat and tol' me never to darken his door again. That's all ri' with muh. His blooming door was dark enough anyway. Then I waltz back to where Wilbur and the gentleman are and break the news. Wilbur gets sore, for since I commenced wearing those pink tights he doped out a great dramatic career for me. And naturally he was vexed. For he saw no show of being able to lay off work.

"Wilbur started to chide me. I was in too gra' a nervousness state to be chid' an' I tol' him sho. Did he have compassion and pity on muh in my vis-vis-situdes? No! Abso-o-o-lutely no! I says all ri' old top, if you look at it that way I guess I can bear up through the heat of the day without your assistance, an' if it's just the same to you I will toddle ri' along and peddle my matches.

"Wilbur pricks up his ears at those few words and tries to copper his remarks, but not for a minute could I see through the fog.

"I just gather up my skirt and sweep majestically out of the room, jump into taxicab and proceed to hunt pleasure and relaxation. What do you know about that?

"Ah! here is the little waiter with his shining morning face. Get me another one of the same and keep your eagle eye on these gentlemen's mugs and see that they do not get dry. Say, take it from me, if I felt any better I'd break out in a rash. I abso-o-o-lutely have no regard for the future. I don' care whether school keeps or not, and Curfew can ring her young head off for all I care. I am going to make old Omar feel like a temperance lecturer before I get through this celebration. I am willing to drink everything but 'Merry Widow' cocktails, for they make you want to steal your own clothes.

"I was expecting to enjoy a box at Ted Marks' big pow-wow at the New York this afternoon, but I fear me at about that time the only thing I will be in condition to attend will be the usual hang-over party in the Metropole.

"Mr. Marks is sure the one clever party. He's going to organize a club called 'The Human Nightkeys.' Any one that goes to bed before daylight is barred. Lee Harrison offered his services as sergeant-of-arms to see that the rule is observed.

"Now that Summer is coming on this sleep question is getting shoved off in a dark corner by itself. It always was a waste of time.

"I don't care a whoop for the best man that breathes and now that I have slipped Wilbur the go'-by I shall never fall in love with one of his sex again. Tell muh, do I look all ri'. I haven't detailed the rest of this adventure, have I? Well, I left Wilbur and met a nice quiet party that was singing 'We're Afraid to Go Home in the Dark' over in Jack's and I at once began to mingle. They were all good fellows, so I nearly gave them heart trouble by ordering wine for the crowd.

"I will not endeavor to chronicle the amount of lush I tucked away. I will only state that if I had not been a good friend to the bell hops I never would have gotten upstairs.

"Estelle, that's muh maid, was sitting up with her face to the pane waiting for me to come home, and just to show her how grateful I was I gave her all of Wilbur's pictures and all the change I had in my stocking. Waiter, you are forgetting your duties in part.

"I finally got to bed and then I pulled off the big cry. Booze, you understand, and not because I lost that hot-air shooting, lush-working, expense-account-grubbing wah of a Wilbur. I should say not. Don't think that I wear pink tights and can't get the best man that ever breathed.

"I am not a bit like that Glonesganes creature. Why, she actually throws herself at the head of every man she meets. Honest, you can't take her out to supper in a crowd before she's engaged to some two or three in the party. Fact. Ask any of the girls. We all swore to tell the same story about her.

"Am I going back on the stage. Well, I should hope so, dear. What do you think I would do with myself if I didn't have to beat it to the shop at least once a day. I tried it once when I first got my fortune, but life became so monotonous and I got so fat that I had to start rehearsing in order to get back to my former self.

"Say, I think the last dipperful made me feel better. Waiter, come out of your trance. Gee, but I do feel great.

"Won't you all have a little something to eat. A steak smothered in pickles or something like that. Go as far as you like. You know I ain't that kind of a girl. When I'm treating there's no entries scratched. Go ahead do as you please. I ain't going to get married, so I don't have to save my money.

"You just watch Wilbur hedge. I got spies out and they say he's been in every cafe in town looking for me. Wants to make up. Watch little birdie here. If he comes monkeying around me again I'll pick up one of these and knock him clean out from under his hat. Trifler. How I ever fell for him certainly gets me. How anybody could love a press agent or an actor gets me for that matter. I have been crossed in love and am running no more chances.

"I shall never get married. Never! That statement is for publication. I shall live in peace and quiet near some good cafe and drown my old age in mixed drinks.

"You needn't think I am soused, but I am going to tell you this. Unless Wilbur and I make up the Friar Festival will have to get along without my services. Why, I got every John in town so bunked that every time they see me coming they take it on the run for some place that I can't get to 'em, 'cause I lance 'em for a pair of seats every time our trails cross.

"I lost eight dinner engagements last week just on that account and what do I get for it? Ice water. That's all.

"Wilbur rushes up and demands more seats and the committee thinks he is having an awful rush of business and its muh with my shoulder to the wheel. I had a run in with Wilbur already about the Friar Girl that Harrison Fisher drew on the front of the programme. Wilbur told me that I could have the job and I finds out that he told everybody in the company the same thing. Press agents is crafty people. And he can play both ends against the middle in a manner that would make your hair curl.

"I don't care! I don't care! Wilbur can run and make faces at himself. Nothing bothers muh. Waiter, are you asleep at the switch? I am no longer a fiancee. I am a free woman.

"Say, what'yer going to do 'morrow? Let's get one of these taxicab things and see if we can't run it to death.

"I never found the limit yet on one of those gasmeter attachments, an' I am the inquisitive soul. Line out to Claremont or some of those foolish places. Sure, we'll start early, about noon, and enjoy the beautiful Spring-air and highballs. Are you on? Sure I'll be there with my hair in a braid. I am the Rural Kid these days and a stunt like that suits me from the ground up.

"Who is that coming in the door? Why, its Wilbur! He sees me! Do I look all ri'? Here, Wilbur, here. Sit down and have a drink, dear, I have been looking for you everywhere. Forget that deal last night. So long fellows. Waiter give me the check; I don't care what becomes of my money now."

Sabrina gives an automobile party to several of her friends so that they may enjoy the country air, but after investigating the atmosphere carefully the opinion of the entire party is that the only healthful ozone is that that comes out of a champagne bottle.

CHAPTER SIXTEEN

"Where you all going?" demanded a voice, and looking around we discovered Sabrina, the Show Girl, and two of her girl friends seated in a big red automobile that was drawn up to the curb. "Come on, jump in," she continued. "We are out to commune with nature for a few minutes and you might just as well be a commuter as the rest of us. Ain't this the one grand weather?

"No, you sit back here. We will make Wilbur sit up in front so that we can see he don't grub the eats. He's inside lancing the management for a group of free lunch and a package of liquid refreshments. Here he comes now. Bless his young heart he's got his arms full. Ain't it grand to be loved by such a man?

"No, Wilbur, you get up in the hurricane deck and we all will sit in the caboose. Have we got everything? Alla, did you forget the hot-water bag full of cracked ice for the champagne? Now, let's see where shall we go first to get the most nature? We can stop at the Cadillac, the Circle, the Casino in the Park and then make a quick jump to Claremont.

"In that way we can get some of the delightful Spring air and not be far from a head waiter at any time. Thats right, Sadie, you big gump, put your feet on the crackers. Those were bought to eat and not to be used as a door mat. Still, if you must wipe your feet we can print 'Welcome' on one of the crackers and you can clean your Dorothy Dodds till you are black in the face.

"Is everything ready? Do I look all right? Wilbur, give the motorman two bells. Look out, there! There goes Er Lawshe with a plaster cast of Genee under his arm. Do you want to make him drop it and break his heart?

"Sadie, it is not necessary to give the furtive glance to every gentleman who admires the machine. Go ahead and see if you can't scrape the paint off the cop. Alla, my dear, you know it isn't necessary to start eating now, you'll get yours, and besides several of the places we will stop at have free lunches, so you can have all that you are accustomed to without making inroads on the provision supply at this stage of the game.

"What 'a we got in the larder? Fifteen bottles and 10 cents' worth of crackers. My! it seems to me you are squandering an awful lot of money on food. Of course, if we get shipwrecked or something they may come in handy, but at present writing they are excess baggage.

"Whoa, chauffeur! Don't you see that bock beer sign? Whenever you see one of those turn the corner and stop at the family entrance. Hitch the machine and we will all soon see what mine host has in the way of nourishment. Sadie, it is not necessary to show such unseeming haste, as it is now but early noon and the place does not close until after midnight.

"This is a low-browed dump, but any port in a storm, as the poets say. As I am directing this Cook's tour we will have but one drink here.

"Wilbur, how do you know that the bar-keeps name is George? Have you been false to me and been here with another? Bartenders are called George just like Chinamen are called John? What are you trying to bale out to me? Do you think I am a boob?

"Now, Alla, go to it and quench your thirst, for it may be several blocks before we stop again. My, ain't this warm weather glorious! It makes one so thirsty. Come, people, let's get back in the herdic, for we have a long journey ahead of us.

"There you go again, Sadie. Stepping all over the crackers. Before we get through we will have to take them in capsules. Look out for that car! Gee, those cars are bad enough without being mashed up more by some sneeze wagon. Certainly we'll go through the Fifth avenue entrance to the park. I may be some things, but I am no piker, and, besides, we got as much license as anybody. I remember when I used to go horseback riding through here every morning and I always had my groom in a beautiful red livery following me. I had the most beautiful black horse and an elegant riding habit. Why, there wasn't a day but what I was invited out to lunch. Sadie, that was very uncalled for. I am in no trance. You, of course, not being accustomed to those things, naturally look upon those people who were brought up on such stuff as balloon juice merchants. Maybe that will make you stand hitched.

"Look at that hearse go by us. Driver, if you are any good you will make that outfit look as if they were bound to the bannister.

"That's right, give them a touch of high life. Zow-e, if we are going less than a mile a minute I hope I have to walk home. Cheese, there's a bike cop.

Can you loose him? Beat it. Good-by, Bobby. Look out, there's another one in front. Slow up, for goodness sake, or we will be pinched. What is it, sergeant? Oh, no, sir. Not more than six miles an hour, I am sure.

"This machine has got a dudedad on it that prevents it from going more than ten. Won't you have a little drink, officer? Just smile on the gent in the front seat; he's right there with the distillery. Wilbur, chase the roof off a jug of suds for the Lieutenant. I tell you, Captain, on my honor as a lady, we are not going more that six miles an hour. Must take us to the station! Why, you low-down, monkey-faced excuse for a sparrow cop, would you have the crust to stand up in front of a judge and tell him that we were going faster than ten miles an hour? If you want to get us to the station it's a cinch you will have to push the machine. Walk! Not so you could notice it. The only way you can get me there is to drag me by the hair of my head, and if you dare lay your mitts on my new marcel wave I will report you to your Commissioner, and if a certain friend of mine don't stand strong enough with him to have you broke, I'll eat my ostrich plume!

"Will let us go if we promise not to do it again? Why, certainly we won't, Sergeant. Thank you, Lieutenant. Here's a little something for the Relief Fund. Good-by, Captain. Wilbur give the driver two bells. The nerve of that guy thinking he could pinch me. I'll have you know that I am only nicked by the best cops on Broadway, and not by any high-grass constable. Hand 'em salve, pardy, hand 'em salve. A soft answer turneth away wrath. If that don't turn the trick use a brick.

"Oh, gee, there it is. Go around and come up the other side so we can be seen from all the tables.

"Let's take this table. Waiter, get on the job, as these gentlemen and ladies wish to address a few remarks to you. Oh, there's Grace McSweeney. Pipe the hat she is sporting. Bum taste, it strikes me. Who is that slob with her? Oh, hello, dear! I was just speaking of your new hat to Sadie. We both admired it so.

"We were wondering how you could wear it coming up on the Subway. I've found that the wind blows them all to pieces in my car. Who's the wop? From Pittsburg? Oh, is that so? He reminds me so much of a very dear friend of mine that was sent up for life. No, I suppose it's not the same party, though they are as alike as two peas. No, I don't care to meet him. You know one in my position cannot afford to associate with every Tom, Dick and Harry. Must you toddle? Good-by, dear.

"Cat! Did you get wise to the way I slipped her the sassy roast? Well, here's down the Irish channel. Varlet, fill up the flagons again. I just love to sit here and look out at Nature and the railroad tracks and the brick scows.

"Where do we go from here? You made me think I was back in the business. Oh, I don't care. Yonkers, over in Westchester County, or we can take the ferry for Jersey if you want to go out in the wilderness. It makes not an iota of difference to muh. Just as long as the chauffeur stays sober. Shall we hike? Lets slip up the drive for a ways. Sadie, are you ever going to have sense enough to keep your hoofs off those crackers? Honest, I don't believe your think tank is feeding properly. Why don't you blow in it and clear it out?

"Sure, I'll caper out to Yonkers if the rest of the crowd want to. I am just that kind of a fellow. Ain't I, Wilbur, dear? Oh, my, don't for mercy sakes disturb him. He's hunting locations for the Friar three-sheets that Mr. Gillen slipped 'em. He's got Mr. McManus' art studies planted now so that the burg looks like a Kansas town the day after the number two car of the circus leaves.

"Did you know that they are enlarging the secret tunnel in the new Friary so that Toxen Worm can get his getaway if the occasion should arise? Honest, it looks like the front view of the Hoboken tunnel. Oh, law me, what is that in the offening? Eureka! It's another cafe, or do muh eyes deceive me? I am athirst, let us rest our weary beast and partake of a flagon of nut brown ale. Say, I guess I would be bad in this Shakespeare thing. Alight, fair maids, and nominate your idea provokers.

"Waiter, follow those people's directions and do not let the mice build nests under your feet. Sink this and we will then continue our journey.

"Now, Sadie, as a friend I ask you don't do a ballet on them crackers. Run over the mutt. What care we for life. Gee, the canine is right there as the artful dodger. Ah! what? Bing! What was that? A puncture! My! For goodness sake, how long will we be bogged down. Oh, we can wait that long, can't we, dears? Pipe the yokel. Shall I hand him a game of chatter? No? Oh, very well.

"Let's have a picnic. Wilbur, get on the job and skid out the liquids. Alla, you may bring out what is left of the crackers. If that woman hasn't paraded over them biscuits until there isn't a piece there big enough to make a nice comfortable mouthful for a young flea.

"Throw 'em away, we don't want to overload our stomachs anyhow. Can you surpass that for a man. Here we've come all these weary miles carefully nursing these bottles to our bosoms and then that excuse there has the crust to speak up and say, 'I forgot the corkscrew.' Can you beat it? Wilbur, you just get on the job and pull them out with your teeth. Get away, you big standup and fall down, I'll show you how to get them out. What do you think us fair sex wear hat pins for, hey, shover? Want some of this jig juice for your tire? Right-o! Ain't I the English scamp? Got her fixed all right? Climb in, folks, and we will journey homeward, for I am beginning to feel thirsty and you certainly don't get the same treatment here that you do in town. Sadie, now that the crackers are gone I wish you would please remember that that is my foot. Say, you can never learn some of these dolls nothing. Nothing personal, my dear, though your hair is light.

"Don't you dish me out any hectic language, for I am a lady. I might forget myself and smear one all over you. Wilbur, are you going to sit up there and see your near-bride insulted by a woman? If you don't come back here and make her stop abusing me I'll take and bump your two hearts together. Now that goes if you hear it and I am speaking in no whisper.

"Can that fight talk even if this is a pleasure party. My, how time does fly! We are nearly home now. Let's all go down the street and see what's doing. Must you leave us? Don't rush away in the heat of the forenoon. So long. My, I am glad that man's out of the machine!"

Sabrina, in spite of the anti-betting law, goes to the race track and returns with money. She also drops a few remarks concerning gentlemen who claim their scarf-pins have been purloined by ladies.

CHAPTER SEVENTEEN

"Them Senators that put the kibosh on that racetrack bill can consider themselves as personal friends of every chorus Fluff that ever scanned a dope sheet," remarked Sabrina, the Show Girl, as she alighted from a new big automobile. "Pipe the ferry-boat. It's all mine; name on every piece. And I am personally thankful to those gents that I am the proud possessor of the same.

"Did I catch? Well, I should hope so, dear. I landed this buzz wagon out of a ten dollar pike bet. Can you surpass it? Talk about playing in luck. Wait until I touch wood. Wilbur says betting on the races beats trifling with the affections of an expense account all to pieces.

"You know that, though I lead a simple and uneventful existence, the inheritance that was left me was pretty near all in, and it was either up to me to get married, get a job on one of the roofs or catch a live one, and I thought the best of all the evils was to catch the aforementioned live one. I am not one of these Janes that goes dotty over the pit-i-pats, and though I always sit up until The Morning Telegraph comes out on the street, the racing news is not the first thing I turn to.

"Wilbur's show closes in a couple of weeks and he is going to the island for the summer. Can that old stuff. I mean Coney, not Blackwell's. I been piking around for a hunch for some time, and just the other evening I was out with a party who is interested in the bet placing business at all of the big tracks, and he said he was hep to a few killings, and any time I would come out he would give them to me and I could play the other books.

"Knowing that he had influence, I naturally took an interest in him, but, say, this is a long, sad story and—. Ah, certainly! I knew you could not suppress your Southern hospitality much longer—that is, I hoped you couldn't. Yes, waiter; bring me a long one.

"Well, I took a peep at my check-book about a week ago and decided that it was me for the track. I meets this wop and he certainly lands me in right. He gives me a twenty case note and the card. I got the twenty changed and plants ten of it in the Lisle Thread Bank, making up my mind that no matter what happened the day would not be ill-spent.

"I plays his tip at 8 to 1 on the first race and ketches. Out of that ninety I plant forty. Still following the kind gentleman's advice I pikes the fifty on a dog in the second race and he never does come in.

"Can you beat that? This betting person picks the whole card but this one race. I lose my fifty and was thinking seriously of going home when I got a yen to try it again, so I dug up a twenty out of the hose. Honest, it nearly broke my heart to separate myself from that roll, but I just had to do it. I get twenty to one, go into hysterics at the quarter, faint at the half, but come to in time to see my money coming in so far ahead it looked as if he was out for a pleasure trip. Can you see me with that 400 in my mit? Talk about throwing fits. Why, I had the Leamy Ladies looking like children romping on the nursery floor.

"There was nothing to it. I had a hunch to grab the bundle and beat it for home and crawl under the bed. And then I had another hunch that told me to stick for the big show. I plant one century in my war bag and get seven to two on the next with the other three. I win.

"Then I do want to go home. I felt ill.

"But just then a gentleman introduced himself to me and we went and had a little drink. That made me feel better, and so I ditched the purveyor of refreshments and fled to the clubhouse. There is nothing more to tell except that I couldn't lose and I came home in an automobile with my clothes so full of this evergreen stuff that I looked as if I had spavins or something else.

"I made $6,000 on the day, which is not so bad for a poor fluff like me. That night the gentleman who gave me the tips called me up and wanted his original twenty back, saying the public got all his roll. Can you beat that? I told him I thought he was a moonstone sport, and to never darken my door again.

"He needed money bad, and through a friend I let him have a couple of thou on this machine. Ain't I the business woman?

"Wilbur and I have just been riding ourselves to death ever since. He has been acting awful lately. Ever since he heard that Friar Weber and Friar Field were going to appear together at the festival he has been soused. It was all I could do to restrain him from kissing Phil Mindel in the Cadillac the other evening. He just don't care what he does.

The Sorrows of a Show Girl: A Story of the Great "White Way" | 85

"Have you bought your tickets? Let me see. I have six choice ones here in the seventh row. You'll want to bring your family, of course, 'cause it will be the chance of a lifetime. Nothing like it seen before under one canvas. For stellar attractions it's going to have Barnum & Bailey's looking like a Sunday school entertainment. Yes, sir, and I personally will be there like the Trinity chimes.

"Alla McSweeney has gone and blown herself for one of these racecourse hats. You know these big things that have a half-mile track around the outside. While I do not wish to injure the poor dear, still I will say that she certainly looks one of these long-handled Jap umbrellas. You know she is such a skinny thing! Honest, this new hip style they are boosting this season just saved her life. She was getting saddle galls from carrying so many naturals. I wouldn't say this unless I absolutely knew, and of course I have seen her early in the morning when you haven't.

"There are little confidences us girls exchange in the privacy of our boudoirs that would never do for the ear of a man. She tried to get a job as one of those six-foot girls in 'The Love Waltz,' but the manager told her she had better go with a circus. She naturally queried 'Why?' And he, the rude thing, told her she could get a job as a quarter-pole. That's why she could never get a job with the Held show. She was all right in low neck, but when it came to tights! Well, you know bowlegs never did appeal to the front row.

"Mind you, I wouldn't say a thing that would hurt her character the least bit, but you should have seen the way she carried on when she was out in Chicago. You know that anyone who runs around with those La Salle street spendthrifts loses class, anyway, and she just tore around that North Side something scandalous, and till my dying day I never will forget the scene she and the comedian's wife had on the platform in that dear Peoria.

"Alla, bless her heart, she is a good soul, is a flighty creature and she accepted the attentions of the comedian which his wife was not supposed to be jerry to. But one day some gabby girl put wifey next. We were all down to the station waiting for the train to come in when up romps wifey to this doll, who is making the big talk with a chorus man—just shows you what extent she will go for company—she was talking to this chorus man and wifey capers up to her and says: 'You been flirting with my husband, haven't you?' And hauling off wifey hangs one on Alla's map that is a thing of beauty and a joy forever. Bing goes Alla to the platform down and out. She was in such a trance that we had to rub her hands and borrow a drink from the press agent, who came back with the show to see if he couldn't get his salary, before she would come to. Pale, why that girl was so white that her number eighteen looked like big gobs of red paint on each cheek.

"I never saw a girl so surprised in my life. For the nonce she was nonplussed. She didn't know what to make of it. When she did you should have heard the language she used. It is not for me to tell it in a respectable crowd, for I only use it to Estelle, that's my maid, when she pulls my hair, but it was certainly not fit for publication in a family newspaper.

"She's continually getting into trouble. If it ain't one thing it's another. It's a wonder to me she hasn't been pinched oftener than she has.

"I never will forget one time she was out riding with a handsome gentleman from Pittsburg in a cab and while leaning on his shoulder his diamond scarfpin got caught in her teeth. She being a bashful young thing— then. Well, when she takes her head off his shoulder the pin naturally comes along, too, and then she got afraid that he would think she was trying to nick it so she stuck the pin in her hat band, intending to restore it on the way home. But in the next cafe they stopped in she picked a fight and left him in a huff. Would you believe it, that guy had the nerve to come around the next day and declare that she had pinched the bauble and threaten to land her in the booby hatch if she didn't come across.

"And they call that chivalry!

"No true gentleman would ever threaten to have a lady sent up.

"Did he get his pin? Well, I should say not. She threw such a strong bluff about suing him for defamation of character that he came across with two hundred cold to keep her quiet. But don't breathe this to a soul unless they promise not to tell. I wouldn't have it get out that I ever said anything about her for worlds, for, though we are the best of friends, I am leaving her no opening to hand me one.

"Don't think for a minute that I have a past I am afraid to bring before me. My fair young life has been as quiet and uneventful as an old mill stream. Fact. You see, still water runs deep and the race is not always to the swift. And goodness knows I would have no one say that about me. I'm a Bohemian, whatever that is. Lots of dames I know have pasts. Why, every time you mention Sid Eusons to Laura she nearly coughs up a spasm and to even breathe medicine show to a certain leading man I know he will immediately cut you off his calling list.

"The benefit business is not as prosperous this year as it has been heretofore. I know several parties that have actually lost money on them.

"Now that Lent is over I am going to have a good time. I always observe Lent some way. This year I swore off refusing drinks or suppers. Wilbur and I expect to be made one as soon as he locates his next season's job. He's got one in sight that looks pretty good.

"A certain party has signed for it, but Wilbur gets it if this party drops dead, so now Wilbur is following him around telling him that he looks poorly. We ought to be very happy when we get married, for Wilbur will be out ahead of a show all season and I will be here in New York. What more would a happy bridal couple desire?

"Well, I must toddle along, as the hour is late and my automobile is getting impatient.

"Be good, and don't forget that you promised on your word and honor to take six tickets for the Friar Festival from me. Say, party, if you need any change give me the office and I will slip it to you."

Sabrina makes a few remarks concerning a pink-whiskered bark who is trying to convert the merry-merry and questions the propriety of going on an extended yachting cruise with a grass widow for a chaperone.

CHAPTER EIGHTEEN

"Say" remarked Sabrina, as we reached her table the other evening. "Did you hear the gladsome tidings? Some purple-whiskered bark is going to caper in this country from dear old Lunnon and deal out religion to the Fluffs of the merry merry. Can you surpass it?

"He is going to slip it to us in our tea. Like knockout drops, I guess. Gee, can you see him distributing tracts to that mob. It's a cinch that they will make good curl papers, anyway.

"The only way to convert most of these dames is to wait until the morning after a birthday party and work the remorse gag before they have a chance to get a bracer for their hangover.

"Can you see him taking a bunch of them out on a picnic like he did in England. Claremont or Far Rockaway for theirs, and if he didn't come across with the big feed with the necessary liquid trimmings it would be the tar and feathers for his. I have had several wine agents try to convert me, but I always stick to the same brand. Let him come over and we will show him a time that will make old Pap Dowie's reception look like a twinkle.

"At that, us chorus dames ain't so worse. Of course there are a bunch of shines in the aggregation, but I guess if you kept tab you would find out that about nine-tenths of them slide for home as soon as they get the cosmetic off their eyelashes. It's the other tenth that try to be the human night keys that crab the act for the whole works.

"There's more dolls keeping their little sisters in convents than there is ones buying white-topped shoes. The poor Jane has to go somewhere to make her forget the blooming show shop.

"A bunch of these high-browed clucks jump all over the villages, ladies of the court, etc., and think it's their fault that the price of lobsters is so high.

"Maybe the price of lobsters is high, but did you ever see a chorus girl buy one for herself?

"An actress gets handed hers at every stage of the game, just because a few make the big noise. These old cranks are always laying for a chance to get a little limelight, and they naturally make the big talk about people that are in the public eye, and those that they know nothing about.

"They should either furnish those guys with a muzzle or give them a pike at the inside of the show business so that they would either keep their trap shut or know what they are talking about. I will admit that there are some grand wonders in this business, but that is no reason why the whole game should be crabbed, and all get the pan for the actions of a few.

"You all know that I am broad minded. I believe that everybody should have a good time if they can keep sober. Of course I don't mean painfully sober, but not to get disgustingly disgusting so that they have to be dragged to the taxi. That I call going too far, and entirely unnecessary.

"If a fluff commences to get too moist around the lamps she should either plead a headache and slide for the curled hair or throw her drinks on the floor when the host is holding hands or exchanging quips with one of the other ladies in the party.

"Drink is an awful thing, especially the next morning. Thanks to Wilbur's teaching, I take a spoonful of olive oil every evening before I duck the hut, so I can sit in with the best and have the seating capacity of a bonded warehouse.

"I pray thee do not breathe these little maidenish confidences, for it might make hard feeling between me and some of my gentlemen friends I have had to get checked at numerous places of refreshment.

"Wilbur is so busy getting ready for the Friars' Festival that you can't chase a word out of him about anything else. Mr. Erlanger, Lee Schubert, Lew Dockstader and Fred Thompson have all kicked in for their boxes, and it is expected that a few more will realize the merits of the attraction and kick in this week.

"To see the paper they have had given to them you'd think it was the storeroom of the Bailey Show.

"I ain't saying nothing, but you just wait until those guys get through with the long-handled brushes. They are going to give Friar Green the job of tacking cards because he is quick on his feet. The big festival comes off next Thursday, so if you haven't bought your seats it's time to get busy. It will be the one best bet in the show line this season.

"Just think, Mr. Weber and Mr. Fields are going to appear together for the first time in years.

"Honest, I am so excited over the affair that I can hardly wait. Wilbur got two seats in the first row, and I'll be there with new frock on, my hair in a braid and my feet in the orchestra pit. Between the festival and the new clubhouse it's got Charley Cook running around in circles. And Wells Hawks is so busy doping out stuff that I saw him pass an elephant the other day without speaking to it.

"Harry Alward is working three eight-hour shifts every day, and the whole blooming gang have gone so noodley that they won't even stop to buy me a drink, and you can take it from me that when those guys overlook a chance to do something for somebody in distress something has gone wrong, or there is a big hen on.

"What was I talking about? Oh, yes. Have you heard the latest gossip? Alla McSweeney is wearing 'Merry Widow' cocktails on the outside of taxicabs now. That poor dear has to swallow a sinker with everything she inhales. And she always comes up bright and cheerful with her face to the pane waiting for the next one. I've seen her go under four times in an evening, and though a little pale she is always there with the chimes when the curtain drops.

"Yes, I put on my light ones some two weeks ago. I got jerry that there would be some class to the humidity, so I made the quick change.

"I cannot decide yet what to do for the summer. I don't know whether to go down to Bath Beach and take a cottage, go to the mountains or go back to Emporia for a trip. I got run out of that hick hamlet the last time I was there, and I am afraid if I go back I might get lynched. You can never tell what those emotional tillers of the soil are going to do next. Why, they are just as liable to vote for Bryan as not.

"I have been invited out to Far Rockaway for a week or two. Mr. Corse Payton is going to make his summer home out there, and if he is within a radius of ten miles I know we are slated for the one grand time. He is so full of Iowa gallantry that he wouldn't let even a dog go by without offering it a highball. He's just that soft hearted. He's got a young hotel out there and the bars are down for any of his friends.

"Some of us girls are talking about getting a houseboat and leading the simple. The chances are it will fall through most everything we dope out does. That's the trouble with us actresses. We get a wild idea and work it to death for a few minutes and then somebody says, 'I'll buy,' and the stuff is off. We could have lots of fun on a houseboat if it had a cool cellar. I certainly do love to go bathing by moonlight. It's so romantic.

"There's a certain party of some prominence on Wall Street that wants me to be one of a party on board his yacht, as his wife is going to Europe for the summer, but I don't know about these yachting parties, for there has been so much scandal about some of them that I am afraid it will lacerate my reputation. You know, above all things, I must be careful with that. Especially now that I am going to become a bride. Yep, Wilbur and I expect to pull off the wedding bell specialty early in June, or as soon as the season opens at Saratoga.

"I think a young married couple can have such a nice quiet time in Saratoga if they go there on their bridal trip and the season is opened. There is so many society people and others there that life never drags.

"I remember I was there on my first wedding tour, but my husband wasn't with me. What! Didn't you know I had been married. Certainly I have, and I am betraying no confidences when I declare myself. Yes, I have been married, and to Saratoga on my wedding trip my husband couldn't accompany me because he was with another show. I never had such an extended bridal trip. All one-night stands. I was with a musical comedy at the time, and I met my husband in Racine, Wis. I know that's an awful place to meet anybody, even your husband, but this is a sad and true tale. He was the leading juvenile with a one-two-three show, and such a handsome thing you never saw on the stage.

"Honest, to hear him spring that sure-fire hokum you would have thought he believed it. I know he passed the same line of dope out to me, and I fell for it. What more could you ask? I was a young and trusting thing then, having been in the business only one season, so I was not 'wised' up to the proper point to believe no man until he makes good. He introduced himself to me after the performance, and as we were laying off there waiting for the angel to come across with the necessary funds for us to continue our successful tour, I had nothing else to do but to listen to his line of chatter.

"He handed it over so strong that I took it all in, and one day when he sought my hand I nailed him to the mast and we beat it for the justice of the peace and were made one.

"His show closed shortly after that and I had to learn to send him money. He got so proud and stuck up that he wouldn't even hunt for a job, until at last it got so unbearable that I had to get a divorce.

"He was a gay and festive young thing, and though I left town the day we were married I still look upon him as my first husband.

"No, I never have seen him since, but we did a great deal of corresponding especially when he needed money.

"If you could get Clarence—yes, that was his name ain't it a scream?—if you could get Clarence soused he was the boy comic. Honest, I have seen him bring a smile out of a head waiter.

"He was the real spendthrift. Why, every day he was courting me in Racine he would take me down and let me look at the lake for hours at a time, and often he would tell me he was going to take me boat riding. Shows what a piker I was. If I knew what I do now I would have sprung a laugh and told him if he wanted my fair young heart he would have to show me more excitement than a watch meeting.

"My, how I do run on! Here I got to sell a couple more seats for the festival, for it is coming off a week from this coming Thursday, and I want to have all the other girls faded. What, must you go? Say, party, take it from me—break open your bank and count your pennies, for it's the chance of a lifetime. Da-da."

She discusses the advisability of chorus girls charging time for their company like a taxicab. She goes for a sail on the river and the party meets with several accidents before finally having a wreck.

CHAPTER NINETEEN

"Gee, Kid, I can scarce restrain myself," remarked Sabrina, the Show Girl, as we met her on the street.

"The big show comes off Thursday afternoon, and me! Why, I'll be there dressed up like a circus. Take it from me, it's a bet you don't want to overlook. I seen a guy go up to the managers and wave $10,000 in their faces for the box office receipts, and all he got was the cold, cruel laugh of scorn.

"The clubhouse had its official opening last night, and as yet none of those that were in attendance have appeared upon the scene. I ain't saying a word, but I bet they had an awful time.

"Them Friars are great people. I been the busy little bee all week trying to get some tickets, but I guess they are all sold out. All of the out-of-town guys are clamoring for gallery seats behind posts. And anything less than $50 for one of the seats is considered as car fare.

"Wilbur went to the opening of the new clubhouse last night, and I got a 'phone from him this morning saying he was going home and get some sleep.

"Say, party, was you up to the Friars' Convention last Sunday? Talk about fun, this sixty laughs in sixty minutes stunt looked like a Methodist watch meeting.

"Honest, I felt sorry for Miss Piatt of 'The Merry Widow' bunch. She was elected to represent that outfit by the whole company Saturday night and then none of the girls showed up to vote for her. The funny thing of the whole works was that Miss Sara Spotted-Weazel from the Bill Show nearly won at that. Gee, did you hearken to the cadenza she turned loose? Indian comic opera. Fine business. I am glad Josephine Cohan got it, 'cause she's a nice girl, though Louise Dresser is all right at that.

"Beban was the foxy guy; every time anybody didn't show up from any company he would claim that he was the delegate and put the thing through. Wasn't Al Davis the busy party! Corbett thought the thing all out and Davis did the hard work, and then every Friar for miles around put in their little gab and told Davis how it should be done.

"Did you ever notice that the party inside the taxi knows more about running it than the chauffeur? Al was wise. He paid no attention to their words of advice and that's why the thing was a success. Too many chefs spoil the cheese sandwich. Them's my words and they go as they lay. Hank Green got sore 'cause I spoke to him, so I won't do it any more.

"Wilbur and I are to be united in wedlock next week and we are going on our wedding tour. Where it will be goodness only knows. It may be only to Canarsie or Far Rockaway.

"Since he met me he has planted a bunch of change, and a gentleman friend of mine gave him a few tips on the market, and he's got what he claims is a tidy sum. He's talking about taking a trip to Europe. Such a chance. What license have we in that neck of woods? I told him to take a ride over the Williamsburg bridge and that would give him all the Europe he wanted.

"He wants to go over there and bring back a couple of big vaudeville acts and make a bunch of money. Rats, I tell him, rats. What does he know about vaudeville acts? Some of these wops that go across never get it out of their systems. All you hear is, 'When I was in London.'

"I remember the time I met Ted Marks in Maxim's. Maxim's is in Paris, you know, my dear. It gives me a sharp, stinging pain. Those burgs ain't such a much. You can get just as good things to drink right here in New York, so, I says to him, 'what's the use of making a fool trip like that?' But he's noodly on the subject and spends half of his spare time reading 'Short Trips in the Old World,' 'Life in the Latin Quarter,' 'Fifty-seven Ways to Avoid Tipping' and all that kind of junk. A trip to Asbury Park would satisfy me just as well.

"Alia McSweeney's Judge gave her a new automobile the other day and we had a match race on the Merrick Road. Honest, the way my car left her tied to the post was a crime. We both stopped drinking three hours before the race commenced, so that our nerves would be in good condition."

"She may be a good chorus girl, but she certainly is a bum racer. I beat her by two dogs, six chickens and a lamp post. I would have got a milk wagon, only Wilbur carelessly blew the horn and scared him up a side street. After the race the loser had to treat the winner to the big eats. I can't tell you what we had, but I can say this much. If she loses another race the Judge will have to go over to the corporations. Eat? We had the best there was.

"Gee, I am sore on this racing thing. You know I went down there a couple of weeks ago and chased the books up a tree. I prance down there the other day and they had me going some. I had a crowd of inside info, and what do I do but let a wop tout me out of it and play his horse. I lost just five hundred cold ones by the deal, and I sure does give this guy a laying out.

"I says to him, 'What license you got to give a lady a bum steer like that? Here I go and plant my fifty on the dog you handed me at 6 to 5, and the 10 to 1 shot I was going to play wins! Where's my comeback? I ask you as a lady, where do I get off?' He offered to kick in with the fifty I lost, but I put up such an awful roar that he gave me two hundred more to ease my aching heart.

"I lose him in the crowd and then take a peek at the entries again and find the gee-gee I intended betting on didn't even start. Of course I couldn't find the party that gave me the two fifty, search as I might. Wasn't that rotten luck?

"I ran that two fifty up to an even thousand before the last race and then beat it for home and mother. The bunch went into the fresh air fund along with the rest. I am now trying to meet some nice gentleman who does business in Wall Street and get him to make a few conservative investments for me. Not that I intend to use any of my own money. Certainly not. But it is a good thing to have a bank account to flash, so that the boob will think he will get a comeback if he does lose.

"A gentleman did put some money up on a margin for me once and then when he got trimmed he came to me for a check and I had to go into hysterics before I could get rid of him.

"The conceited yen some of these boobs have in thinking that a fluff has nothing else to do but sit in some cafe and hold hands until daylight.

"I am trying to get the Chorus Girls' Union to get together and pass a law charging so much for our time, just like a taxicab. Don't you think that would be a good idea? Lots of times the supper ain't worth the time she wastes on the cluck. They could have a little indicator fastened to their Merry Widow hat and as they leave the stage door turn down the flag and not read the meter until he had kissed you good-by in the hall, and then collect. In that way the doll would have the price of breakfast, and maybe a new gag or something for her wardrobe. It would reduce the nightly jam around the stage door by a whole lot.

"Did you hear about the bunch of us going yachting in Gym Bagley's yacht The Hornet the other day? He calls it The Hornet because he got stung when he bought it. The weather was all to the good the other afternoon, so we hike up to Harlem and collar the ship, six of us, and, after loading a bunch of bottled ballast on board, we started out. Gosh, the water was lovely. Gym don't care what becomes of the blooming barge as long as it doesn't get lost. You can even sink it, if you mark the spot. We all leave our Merry Widow lids in the boathouse, 'cause the boat wouldn't hold them, and sallied forth.

"Wilbur said he knew how to sail a boat. Come to find out later, it was a stone boat he had been educated on.

"Well, we elected him the chauffeur and, after hoisting the sail, the gallant craft with its merry-merry crew swung out into the stream. Yo ho, my lads, yo, ho.

"The wind was blowing one way and we wanted to go the other, so after nearly wrecking a couple of tugboats and a brick scow, we fixed the sail so the wind would push the boat right along. Aye, aye, captain, a fish sou'-sou' by east with the wind in his teeth! The sturdy vessel was just tearing along. Honest, you could see it move—right along, just like a clam, when Alla, who, you all know, is the human goat, in trying to reach for a bottle of beer that didn't belong to her, fell overboard.

"It served her right and I told the gang to hit her on the nob with an oar when she came-up. We dragged her in, however, and wrapped her up in a bunch of coats and set her on the front stoop of the craft to dry.

"She got jerry to the fact that there was a bottle of jig juice in the galley and at once threw a chill. Honest, to see that fluff do a stage chill would have made a eel laugh, ha! ha! in that manner. She shook so hard she nearly threw us all out of the scow, so that we finally had to listen to her pleadings and pass her the booze.

"I was for letting her shake so if we wanted mixed drinks al we would have to do was to put the glass in her mitt and say go to it, but some of the gazabos in the mob got a sympathy streak and let her have it. I'd a let her had it, all right, all right, the outside of the bottle right on the marcel.

"The subterfuges these Janes will indulge in to accomplish their ends makes my goat jump the barrier.

"Nothing else marred our pleasant little sail up the river except when we opened the lunch box we found only one sandwich, and no one would eat it. Everybody wanted to trade their interest in it for a bottle of beer, and there was nearly a riot.

"It was finally settled by Wilbur, who is always the fair-haired boy when it comes to emergencies. He took the sandwich and threw it overboard and each and every member of the famished crew had another eyedropper full of suds. If it hadn't been for him, we would be out there yet.

"We had got up to nearly opposite 155th street by this time and some of the less experienced members of the jolly gang were commencing to worry that they would never see Broadway again and stationed a lookout in the bow to find Albany. Aye, aye, the deck, water sighted on the port beam. On duty, captain. These noodley dames were strong for reversing and returning to our harbor, which we had not seen for these many years—ah, the brave sailor lad; alas, he had to remain away from home at night—so Wilbur started to turn the boat around.

"I think he must have thought he was driving a street car, for instead of reversing like any white man would, he pulled off an evolution that was a peach.

"All of the wind ducked out of the sail gag for a minute and the boat spun around, then, all of a sudden, it filled again, and, bingo! the scow slowly lays over on her side an dies. The outfit fell into the water kerplunk. I think I touched the bottom nine times before I grabbed the side of the boat. I remember distinctly of passing a fish so often that we got on speaking terms.

"When I got the briny out of my lamps and took a pike around, there was the whole works clinging to the side of the boat looking like a flock of wet cats.

"The remarks they made to Wilbur I would not repeat here, for he is to be my future husband. The water was as cold as a flat in the Winter time and nothing in sight.

"One of the dames, I wouldn't be surprised if it was that Alla party, suggested that we lash a man to the rigging and let him look for help. Another was strong for turning the flag upside down as a signal of distress. Louie Zweibaum nearly drowned because he had to use both hands to tell her that the rigging was under water.

"We, all between shivers, turned loose a Rebel yell for help and pretty soon along comes a tugboat bound downtown. That drove up alongside and after the captain found out that we had money they hoisted us on deck and took the sloop for a tow.

"Take it from me, I was never so glad to get near a fire in my life. The skipper of the cheese let us get in the engine room and dry out. Can you see that wet bunch of fluffs with all the highlight off and their marcels around their necks. I'll bet there was a whole lot of surprises sprung when the true complexion began to show up. We got fairly well fixed up by the time we got down to where we had to go to get the rest of our stuff and when we once again touched mother earth and the captain of the boat had touched us we took it on the run for a cafe, and let me tell you the market price on hot drinks closed strong in Harlem that night.

"We fixed Gym's boat up and gave it back to him the next day. Nobody caught cold and everything in the garden's lovely.

"Now, dearie, I can call you dearie, for I am soon to be a married woman and it will be all right. Now, dearie, don't forget the big Festival Thursday afternoon, for I will count on your being there to help the crowd.

"Remember the Friars do more for the actors than they are given credit for, so it's up to you to help boost. So long. Don't forget to kick in early and avoid the rush."

Sabrina is married and goes on her wedding trip. Her comments on London and how her husband suppressed several professional gamblers on board the steamer. The two expect to spend some time in England, where we will leave them.

CHAPTER TWENTY

Sabrina was married to Wilbur the day after the Friar Festival and we acted in the capacity of best man and were very much in evidence in the feast that followed. We imprinted chaste salutes on the lips of the blushing bride until the groom tore us asunder. After the festivities Sabrina and Wilbur disappeared and for the past ten days their favorite cafes and loafing places have known them not. We were just beginning to get nervous when the postman brought the following letter:

"London.

"Dear Party—I guess maybe when you pipe off this effusion you will throw a foaming fit and fall in it. Me and Wilbur are now in the city of fogs and take it from me, it's a bum habitation for even a dog.

"After you and the rest of the gang did the shoot the chutes under the table at the wedding breakfast me and his nobs grabbed our make-up boxes and took it on the lope for the ferry station. I thought we were going to take a wedding tour to Asbury Park or some of the other watering places, but what does Wilbur do but sidestep the ferry proposition and we go prancing up to a dock where a boat about nine miles big was hitched and before I had time to give the office to the cop on the beat Wilbur rushes me up the plank and into the outfit. Honest, it was bigger than any of the Coney Island boats. I was under the impression for the nonce that it was the night boat up the Hudson but I didn't see a steward I knew.

"A guy who had enough gilt on to be a Major-General in the National Guard came floundering up and Wilbur gave him his real name and the wop said, 'This way, please, threw us into a young elevator and we went up a couple of stories and along a hall until we came to a door which the gee threw open and said, 'This is your stateroom.'

"Honest, I never saw such a drum. A great big room with a real bed instead of those shelve things and off of the room a bath, and we were only to be on the water five days. Can you beat it?

I was the one surprised pup and as soon as I hung my 'Merry Widow' on the gas jet I asked Wilbur about it.

"He says, 'Kid, we are on the ferry to Europe and we are going to spend our honeymoon across the pond.' I says, 'not for little Sabrina; you don't get her out of sight of New York,' and made a stab for the rail. By the time I got to it we were in the middle of the creek and nothing in sight but a flock of tugboats and a bunch of yaps waving their mitts on the dock. Take it from me, if I hadn't been a bride I would have cut up something scandalous, but it was too early in the matrimonial game to start any lumpy work. So all I did was to sit and pout, 'cause I know I can always make a hit when I flash the pouting number.

"Gee, what could I do? Out there in the middle of the water with a long, slushy walk back to the dock. So I did the next best thing and gave the high sign to the steward to kick in with a few refreshments, which he very graciously did.

"Say, party, I can't tell you how I felt to see little old New York slip away in the distance. That old town is a great old burg, and as I was going to kick into some other country that I wasn't hep to I naturally felt kind of bumly.

"We went busting by the Statue of Liberty and then on out past the Hook, and, take it from me, if that steward hadn't come across with the refreshments just at that moment I would have burst into tears. As it was I could only address Wilbur in a few terse adjectives, and tell him what I thought of a person that would pull off such a low down deal on an unsuspecting fluff. I want to state right now that though I was but a bride I called him good and proper.

"The next morning we went down to breakfast. Say, they have about ten meals a day on one of these scows and I've gained about twenty pounds already. There was a bunch of show people going over on the same boat and Wilbur and I naturally cottoned to them. We didn't do a thing all day but sit on the deck and read, or walk around or sing in the music room. Sure, they got a real live music room on board, as well as a conservatory, a gym and an elevator.

"I don't know whether I plucked a quince or not. Wilbur kept insisting that I go to the table every time they turned in an alarm, and I was sorta holding off, 'cause I didn't want to lance the poor boy for all his change on the way over, but he kept insisting that I eat and acted so peevish when I didn't that I thought, well, if he wants to spend his money all right, so I eat so much that I couldn't have crowded any more in me with a hypo. Come to find out the food was included in the passage and we had to pay for it whether we ate it or not. That's why I am wondering if I plucked a quince. Wilbur was never tight before we were wed, and you can take it from me that if he starts to hold out or draw down now there is going to be fine large doings in the Wilbur family from the female delegation.

"Wilbur was in the smoking room the other evening and got to talking with what he thought were a couple of boobs, but come to find out they were wise guys. After sipping up a couple of slow ones, the guys propose a little poker game. Wilbur and two other boobs fall for the bunk and they open up. Wilbur, after losing a little junk, gives the wise guys the office that he's jerry to the fact that they are playing with newspaper, and lets them know that if he ain't in on the frame-up he'll belch.

"These two boobs are dirty with the evergreen, and Wilbur's got the wise guys so leary for fear he will tip his mitt and they naturally slip him a big one every time they get a chance. Wilbur gets his money back and everything is even all around, but the wise guys are the only ones who want to lay down.

"Wilbur hands them a game of cheerful chatter and they don't dare quit. Foxy Wilbur sits there until 3 a.m., raking in their money, and incidentally corrals some that belongs to the wealthy wops. In the meantime I am doing the earnest conversation act with an old dowager that I met the second day out and she is telling me about her country home in Devonshire or some other one of these shire things. She sorta took a fancy to me and insisted that Wilbur and I should run out there for a week-end. Which end of the week she didn't say. But I guess if we go Sunday we are safe. To hear this old dame tell it, she must own about nine million acres up in the country, and her husband has all kinds of wild animals—lions, tigers, elephants and all that truck that are trained to be shot. She called it a shooting lodge. Probably a branch of the Elks. This old party ceases her harangue and I beat it to the air-felt and am pounding my ear when Wilbur kicks in with a souse on.

"I come out of the hay and am getting ready to call him to a fare-you-well when he flashes his bundle. My anger vanished in a moment and I just reach out and cop the coin and roll over and goes to sleep. Wilbur sleeps on the floor until I took compassion on him and rolled him on the lounge. Talk about your wifely devotion, what! I count the roll in the morning before I slip it to the purser for safekeeping and it assayed $1,245, which is not half bad for a night's work.

"The wise guys come around and offer Wilbur $100 a night to stay out of the smoking room and he won't do it, but tells them if he catches them playing another game during the trip he will turn loose the long Rebel yell. Now the two wise guys are sitting on deck reading 'The Lives of the Saints' and making faces at Wilbur every time he goes romping by. Ain't Wilbur the saucy thing?

"The last night on board we gave a concert for the benefit of the Seamen's Fund, or something like that, and I claim that it was a classy affair. I appeared, and without any brag or ostentation I can truthfully say that I scored a great personal triumph. It wasn't so much what I did, but the winsome manner in which I did it. Get that? Wilbur was the manager of the affair and didn't shake down a cent.

"What do you think of that? He said that a sailor needed all the money he could get and he would be the first man not to take it from them. I made my big hit at the concert in reciting 'Lasca.' One of the mates told me that somebody does 'Lasca' on every trip, but I was the first one that furnished scenery by letting down my hair. I wonder if he was kidding me?

"A great many of the ladies on board spent all their time in playing Bridget whist, and after watching them for a couple of afternoons they offered to teach me the game with a moderate limit. I am hep to this poker thing and can look a pat hand in the face without a quiver of the lip, but I must blushingly admit that I thought I was in for a good old-fashioned trimming when I got up against those dames. It cost me about fifty dollars to learn, and then I had a streak of beginner's luck, and before the whistle blew for dinner I was several hundred to the velvet.

"Two of the Janes put up a horrible holler about it being a friendly game and wanted their money back. I was going to give it to them, because I didn't want 'em to look any older, but one of the others took my part and told me to hold onto the gross. The three that didn't get their's back got out their little hammers and for a while I had no one to talk to but myself or Wilbur, and he was trying to dope out a scheme whereby he could paste threesheets on the ocean and catch the incoming tourists. I left him trying to compose a one-word wireless that would explain the whole proposition to Fred Thompson.

"We came in sight of England or Ireland, or some of those foolish islands, early in the morning, and they didn't look so much. Barren Island has got 'em faded for smell. There were nothing but long white chalk cliffs that a good man with a bucket of whitewash could paint in a week.

"We got into Liverpool and loafed around town for a couple of hours and saw nothing that would cause any excitement. The natives look just the same and dress just the same as they do in America but you have to go some to understand what they say.

"Gee, you should pipe the herdics they use for railroad cars in this man England's country. Instead of making the grand entrance from the end you sneak in at the side and sit in a kind of a pew thing, making faces at some one across the aisle. Wilbur got sore 'cause he blew himself for a couple of tickets and the conductor, I mean, the guard, didn't come around to collect them until we go nearly into London. He wanted to bet an Englishman, on the other side of the hall, $5—Bly me, I mean a pound, that he could make the same trip for nothing and hand the guard a group of chatter that would get him all the way into town.

"When we crawled out of the caboose in London we thought it was midnight, but on asking a cop—my word, I mean Bobby—he said it was nothing but a fog. Wilbur told him that if he wanted him to see much of his blooming city he would have to bring around a dark lantern.

"We called a cab and started for the Savoy. All true Americans when they go to London stop at the Savoy. We drove for about an hour, the horse gumshoeing his way through the dark until we came to the hotel. Wilbur asked the cab driver how much it was and he named the sum that if you even suggested it to a New York cabby he would have you pinched.

"After registering Wilbur called Marcus Mayer up on the telephone. He grabbed down the receiver and after waiting for about half an hour some dame said, 'Are you there?' Wilbur's Nanny took the hurdle and he answered, 'Where did you think I was? Playing pinochle with the King?' After a sharp struggle he managed to get Marcus' hangout, but he wasn't in, so Wilbur started out to hunt the American bar alone. In about fifteen minutes he came back on the run with a couple of Bobbys about two jumps behind him. It seems that Wilbur had found the American bar and walked up to it and asked for a Manhattan cocktail, because he was getting homesick and the bartender said, 'Will you have it made with Scotch or Irish, sir?'

"Naturally Wilbur hit him with the first thing that came handy, which happened to be a heavy beer mug. The bartender was a short sport, and instead of trimming him with a bung-starter, turns loose a yell for the law. So Wilbur lopes on, carelessly knocking over a couple of cops on his way out.

"The two officers that followed him to the room were strong for sending him to the booby hatch, but I had the presence of mind to slip them each a piece of change and they exit laughing. That's all that has happened so far, though we just got in town last night and I am writing this before breakfast. Oh, no; there's something else. Last night Wilbur and I started down to dinner and they shooed him back to put on his evening clothes. He met some of the American bunch after supper, and it took them three hours to tell all the things they did to Georgie Cohan when he was over here. Ted Marks is right here, with his hair in a braid and the white carnation.

"We will stay here for about a week and then caper over to Paris. I got a hunch that Wilbur is fixing to leave me in the outskirts, because I heard him say something about the foolishness of taking a cheese sandwich to a banquet.

"Will write again soon.

"Platonically Yours,

"*SABRINA.*"

"P.S.—Wilbur is in another row downstairs and I got to go and see what's coming off.

"*S.*"